Serial

HOMICIDE

(Book 1)

PLUS 'BONUS' STORY

by: RJ PARKER

Serial

HOMICIDE

(B_{ook} 1)

PLUS 'BONUS' STORY

by: RJ PARKER

ISBN-13: 978-1987902181
ISBN-10: 1987902181

Copyrights

Table of Contents

Chapter 1: Albert Fish

"I like children, they are tasty" - Albert Fish

Albert Fish is led into homicide court by detectives

Albert Hamilton Fish was an American sadomasochistic killer and a human-eater. He was otherwise called the Gray Man, or the Werewolf of Wisteria, or perhaps the Brooklyn Vampire.

Fish was happy to say that he had performed killings in each state, mentioning a number of around 100, although that it wasn't clear whether Fish was discussing an attack or cannibalism, with no way of knowing whether it was a valid number or not. Fish was a key suspect in no less than five killings in his total lifetime. He admitted to three murders that police could follow and to a known manslaughter. He admitted to stabbing no less than two other individuals. He was put on trial for the kidnapping and killing of Gracie Budd and was convicted and then executed by means of the electric chair.

***

He was born in Washington, D.C. in 1870 to Ellen and Randall Fish and was named Hamilton Fish after Hamilton Fish, a remote relative. His father was 43 years older than his mother. Fish was the youngest child with three siblings: Annie, Walter and Edwin. Fish wished to be called Albert after a deceased sibling because he wanted to get rid of the nickname Ham and Egg, as he was called at an orphanage where he spent a considerable period of his childhood years.

Numerous individuals from his family had emotional instability, and one experienced religious madness. His father was a river vessel captain. By 1870, Fish became a compost maker. The senior Fish passed away in 1875 due to a heart attack at Sixth Street Station of the

Pennsylvania Railroad in Washington, D.C. Fish's mother placed him into an orphanage.

While there, Fish was often beaten and whipped, and in the long run, he found that he was liked the physical torment. The beatings would frequently give him erections, and other orphans used to tease him about that.

By 1879, Fish's mother landed a job in the government and could then care for him. Unfortunately, his sundry encounters before that had already influenced him. In 1882, when he was 12 years old, he began a gay relationship with a telegraph boy. Moreover, the boy taught Fish many odd practices such as drinking pee and coprophagy. Fish started going to public washrooms where he watched young men undress, and he spent a good deal of time during the weekends in those places.

By 1890, Fish had gone to New York City where he became a male prostitute. Albert said he started sexually assaulting young men, a crime he continued doing even after his mother found him a wife. In 1898, he married a lady who was a few years younger than himself. They had six children: Eugene, Gertrude, Albert, Anna, Henry and John. Fish was taken into custody for theft and was then sentenced to imprisonment in Sing Sing in 1903. He routinely engaged in sexual relationships with men while he was in jail.

All through 1898, Fish worked as a house painter. According to Fish, he was still assaulting youngsters, mainly young boys under six years old. He later described an episode in which a gay lover took him to the waxworks gallery, where Fish was impressed by a bisection of the penis. Before long, he acquired an aberrant enthusiasm for castration. During a relationship with a retarded man, Fish tried to emasculate him after he had tied him up. The man took fright and fled. Then Fish started to increase his visits to brothels where he could be whipped regularly.

During January 1917, Fish's wife left him and married John Straube, a man who had come to live with the Fish family. After this separation and rejection, Fish started to hear voices. He once wrapped himself up in the floor carpet, saying that he was obeying the teachings of John the Apostle.

***

In 1920, Fish murdered a boy called Thomas Bedden of Wilmington, Delaware. A short time later, around 1919, he wounded a mentally ill boy in Georgetown, an area of Washington, D.C. A large number of his future victims would either be mentally ill or African-

American, as he thought these people would never be missed.

On July 11, 1924, Fish saw 8-year-old Beatrice Kiel who was playing alone on her parents' Staten Island farm. Fish gave her cash to go with him and assist him in searching for rhubarb in the nearby fields. She was just going to leave the ranch when her mother chased Fish away. He left, but he returned afterwards to the Kiels' livestock shelter where he attempted to rest for the night. He was again found by Kiel and told to go away.

Edward Budd, aged 18, was an adventurer who intended to improve himself and escape the poverty of his own parents. On May 25, 1928, the boy placed an advertisement in the Sunday version of a New York newspaper that a young man, aged 18, wishes to get a position to work in the countryside. He gave his address to be Edward Budd from 406 West Fifteenth Street. Edward was a healthy young man who was eager to work in order to add to the prosperity of his family.

He was living in the filthy, stinking, packed city in a wretched apartment with his father, mother, and four siblings. He yearned to work in the countryside where the environment was said to be fresh and clean. The next Monday, on May

28, Edward's mother, Delia, welcomed an elderly man who represented himself to be Frank Howard, a rancher from Farmingdale which was in Long Island, and he said he needed to talk to Edward about a job. Delia sent her 5-year-old daughter Beatrice to get Edward from his friend's apartment. Fish, the old man, offered her a nickel.

Meanwhile, they sat waiting for Edward to return. His mother, Delia, had a chance to take a look at the old man, who had a kind face with silver hair and a dingy, sagging moustache. He disclosed to Mrs. Budd that he had made a living for a long time as an interior decorator in the city, then he retired to a farm he had purchased with his reserve funds. He had six children that he raised without anyone else's input since his wife had left them over ten years ago.

With the assistance of his offspring, five farmhands, and a Swedish cook, the old man had made the farm into a prosperous one with a few hundred chickens and about six dairy cows. One of his farmhands was planning to leave and he required somebody to replace him.

Right then and there, Edward came in and met Mr. Howard, and he commented on the boy's body and strength. The boy ensured that the old man saw him as a diligent employee. Mr. Howard mentioned an offer of 15 dollars a week. Edward acknowledged happily. Howard even consented to employ Willie, Edward's friend.

Mr. Howard needed to leave for a meeting but said he would return on Saturday to take them. The young boys were excited, and the Budds were glad that a decent position with the generous old gentleman had come so rapidly from Edward's humble advertisement.

Saturday, June 2, was expected to be the important day. However, Mr. Howard didn't appear. Instead, they got a note written by Mr. Howard in which he said he had to postpone and would call on them the next morning.

The following morning around eleven o'clock, Frank Howard went to the Budds' house bringing with him gifts such as strawberries and dairy-fresh, velvety pot cheddar. He said that the items came from his ranch.

Delia told the old man to join them for lunch. Thus Albert Budd got the chance to talk to his boy's new boss. It was a talk that left their father exceptionally cheerful. Here was this respectful old man who described his 20 acres of land, his cordial group of farmhands as well as a healthy country life. Albert knew it was the thing that his child needed. On the second visit, Albert consented to contract Budd, and then persuaded the guardians, Delia Flanagan and Albert Budd, to permit Grace to go together with him to a birthday gathering that night at his sister's home. The elder Budd worked as a porter at Equitable Life Assurance. Grace had a sister, Beatrice, as well as two brothers younger than Edward, George Budd and Albert junior. Fish and Grace left together that same day, but never returned.

The police took Charles Edward Pope into custody on September 5, 1930, as a suspect in the kidnapping. The man was a 66-year-old flat administrator, and he was brought to their attention by his alienated spouse. He spent around 108 days in prison from the time of his capture until his trial on December 22, 1930.

The most awful thing that Samuel Dribben, a police lieutenant, said to the Budds was that the address that the fake "Frank Howard" had offered to them was fictional. The compassionate man was a phony. There existed no Frank Howard, no ranch in Farmingdale in Long Island. Nothing he said was valid.

Police started the investigative process. They looked at everything "Frank Howard" said to the Budds. They likewise had the Budds to go over photographs and kept an eye on all known child molesters, mental patients, but they could not trace Gracie.

On June 7, the New York police sent 1,000 fliers to police headquarters all across the nation with a photograph of Gracie and the particulars of "Mr. Howard." The movement, alongside all the local attention, ensured a pandemic of Gracie crackpot letters. Each had to be researched by the 20 or more criminologists who had been placed on the case.

There existed two or three strong pieces of information. Policemen located the Western Union office in Manhattan where "Frank Howard" sent messages to the Budds, in addition to the first written message. An analysis of the writing and grammar indicated that "Howard" had some training and refinement. Police additionally found the push cart from where "Howard" had purchased the pot cheddar he gave to the Budds. Both locations were in the East Harlem area that later then turned into a point of convergence of serious investigations.

A boy named Billy Gaffney, age 4, was playing in the corridor outside his family's flat in Brooklyn with a 3-year-old friend named Billy Beaton. Both of them vanished. Beaton was later found on the roof of the same apartment. When the boy was asked about Billy Gaffney, he said that a boogeyman took him away. Peter Kudzinowski was suspected of the murder of

Gaffney. At that point, Joseph Meehan, a driver for the Brooklyn trolley, had seen a photo of Fish in the daily paper.

He recognized Fish as the man that he had seen on February 11, 1927, who was attempting to calm a young boy sitting with him on that trolley. The boy wasn't wearing a coat and was sobbing for his mother. He was then dragged by the old man off and on the trolley. Policemen matched the good description of the child to Billy Gaffney. His body was never seen again. Gaffney's mother attempted to get additional information about her child's death.

In the long run, somebody listened to the three-year-old witness who gave an account of the boogeyman. The man was thin with silver hair and a drab moustache. The police gave careful consideration to that description but never associated it with a crime which had been claimed by the Gray Man a couple of years before.

In another case in July 1924, eight-year-old Francis McDonnell was playing on the front veranda of his home in Charlton Woods, a part of Staten Island. The boy's mother sat nearby, nursing her newborn child, when she saw an elderly man with silver hair and moustache on the road. She gazed at the old man who kept clenching and unclenching his hands and muttering to himself. That man tipped his dirty hat to her and vanished down the road.

Later that evening, the old man was seen again with Francis and four other young men as they played ball. Fish, the old man, called to Francis come over to him. The others kept on playing, and a couple of minutes after that, both the old man and Francis had vanished. A neighbor saw a boy that looked just like Francis strolling that evening into a wooded territory with an elderly silver-haired man behind him.

Francis's absence was not realized until he later missed supper. His father, a policeman, began a search. Then they found the boy in a forested area under some branches. He had been assaulted. His garments had been ripped away from his body and he had been choked using his own suspenders. He had been beaten so badly that police questioned whether the "old man" could truly have been as old as he looked. The damage was severe to the point that they thought that the old man must have had an associate who had great strength to beat the boy.

***

Albert Fish, as anyone might expect, was not a stranger to the police. His record extended back to 1903 when he had been imprisoned for robbery. From that point forward, he had been brought in six times for different violations; for example, sending indecent letters and insignificant burglaries. Half of those captures happened around the same time as Gracie's kidnapping. Each time, the charges were rejected. He had been in mental facilities more than once.

A youthful janitor came forward and admitted that he took some sheets of paper and some envelopes. He then left the stationery in his prior lodging at 200 East 52nd Street. The landlady said that Fish told her that he was awaiting a letter from his son. The son was in the Civilian Conservation Corps located in North Carolina, and he used to send money to his old father. The post office later informed the detectives that they were holding the letter for Albert Fish. Fish had not recently contacted the landlady, and this worried the police because they thought that something might have scared Fish away.

On December 13, 1934, the landlady called Detective King. At that moment, Fish was in the room looking for his letter. When King opened the door, Fish was sitting holding a teacup. Fish stood, and when King asked if he was Albert Fish, he nodded. Instantly, Fish felt for a razor that was in his pocket, but King grabbed the old man, then twisted his hand sharply and captured him.

Albert Fish's confession was heard by a great many law enforcers. It seemed incredible because the old man appeared innocent. King conducted the first confession when Fish told him that, in the summer of 1928, he had become bloodthirsty. The time he answered to Edward's employment request, he had intended to take him to a remote area and cut off his penis, leaving him to bleed to death.

After he had left the Budds' house, Fish bought the tools he would require to murder and mutilate the boys. He had a cleaver and saw and a butcher's knife. He had wrapped all these tools together and left them at a newsstand, then he went to the Budds' home the second time. Once he saw the size of Edward and his friend Willie, Fish knew they could have overpowered him. However, he had adequate experience to handle them. However, after seeing Gracie, he changed his plan concerning the boys and took Gracie instead.

When he went away with Gracie, he stopped at the newsstand to pick up his packet of tools. Then he took a train to the Bronx and later to a village located in Worthington. It should be noted that he bought a one-way ticket for Gracie. Grace was thrilled by the 40-minute ride into the countryside. Because she had seldom been out of the city, this visit was such an adventure to her.

Fish was carried away by his murder plan and he forgot to take his tools, leaving them on the train. Gracie, however, noted that and reminded Fish to take his package. After a long walk on a remote road, they arrived at an abandoned house called the Wisteria Cottage. The house was located in the midst of a wooded area. Upon her arrival, Gracie began to play with the flowers. Fish went up to the second floor of that house where he spread open his package and then removed his clothes.

He then called Gracie to come up upstairs. Once she saw the man naked, she screamed and tried to escape. Fish quickly grabbed her by the throat and choked her to death. He was sexually aroused by the act. He propped up Grace's head on a bucket and decapitated her. He trapped most of her blood in the bucket and then threw the bucket out into the yard. After undressing Gracie, he began cutting up her body using a cleaver and a butcher's knife.

He took some of the body parts and wrapped them using a newspaper. He left the rest there, only to return some time later to dispose of the remaining parts. He got rid of his tools at the same time. After his confession, King asked him why he did this act. Fish replied that he couldn't account for it.

After being asked the reason for his written letters, he claimed that he had a mania for writing. The same day, the police officer headed to the Wisteria Cottage to recover Gracie's remains. Fish stood nearby and seemed to be devoid of any emotions. Later that night, Fish was interviewed by the Assistant District Attorney. He was asked why he murdered Gracie. He claimed that it was a sort of a blood thirst that had overwhelmed him.

He also claimed that he felt sorrow after the act and that he would have offered his life to recover Gracie's. He said nothing to suggest that he was involved in cannibalism as is clearly shown in the letter to the Budds. The police thought that if they incorporated the act of cannibalism into the case, that would lead to an inevitable defense case for insanity. During that night, the news of his arrest was all over the newspapers. King drove Mr. Budd as well as Edward to the station in order to identify Albert Fish. They were astonished to realize that Fish was not who he appeared to be.

Fish was not new to the police because he

had previous cases of grand larceny. Moreover, since 1903, Fish had been arrested six times for some sort of crimes. All this happened around the time that Gracie was abducted. The charges against him were repeatedly dropped. Fish had visited mental facilities more than once.

Finally, the police had a break. A motorman who saw the picture of Fish in the papers identified Fish as the man he saw on February 11, 1927, carrying a boy on a trolley. The boy cried for his mother, and this confirmed that Fish was also involved in the kidnapping case of Billy Gaffney.

Fish later confessed things about this kidnapping. He said that he brought Gaffney to the Riker Avenue dumps where there was an abandoned house. There he stripped him naked, tying his hands and legs. After undressing him, he burnt his clothes and gagged him using a piece of rag from the dump. The following day, he picked up his tools and cut the boy up. Fish described how he cooked parts of the boy and ate them.

Later, a Staten Island man came to identify the man that had tried to lure his little daughter into the woods. The daughter came to the cell and identified Fish. Fish was additionally connected to the 1932 killing of a young girl named Mary O'Connor. The girl's body was found near a house which Fish had previously painted.

All of these cases were connected to Fish, and this left him with minimal chance of being acquitted. Fish was left with a single chance -- a psychiatrist declaring him insane.

***

Albert Fish's trial for the intentional murder of Gracie Budd started on Monday, March 11, 1935, in White Plains, with Frederick P. Close as the judge and with a Chief Assistant Attorney named Elbert F. Gallagher, a prosecuting lawyer. James Dempsey was Fish's lawyer. The trial went on for ten days. Fish argued madness and insisted he had heard voices from God instructing him to murder the children. A few therapists made statements about Fish's sexual fixations, including coprophilia, urophilia, pedophilia, and masochism. However, there was a difference of opinion with respect to whether these fetishes implied he was crazy.

The defense's central master witness was called Fredric Wertham, a therapist with focus on child improvement who administered psychiatric tests for New York crime courts. Wertham contended that Fish was crazy. Another witness for the defense was known as Mary Nicholas, who was Fish's 17-year-old stepdaughter. She described how Fish showed her and her siblings a game which included hints of molestation and child attack. The jury observed him to be rational and blameworthy, and the judge requested capital punishment.

Grace's parents and sibling Albert, Jr. testified. Dempsey appeared to be resolved to make the point that both Delia and Albert, Sr. gave their consent to Grace going with Fish to the birthday party. When the time came for Grace's father to make his statement, he was overcome with emotions and started to sob.

On the third day of the trial, over the strenuous protests of the defense lawyer, a container of Grace Budd's remaining parts was brought into the court as evidence, while Detective King recreated from Fish's admission how the child was killed. At that point, Gallagher opened a crate and held out the little skull of the dead child. It was an extremely climactic point in the trial.

Dempsey focused on the cannibalism issue as a focal part of the madness defense. Plainly he was attempting to clarify that Fish had eaten parts of the young lady's body - something that any normal individual wouldn't do. In any case, he was unsuccessful in demonstrating that Fish really did what he said he did with her body.

Fish seemed, by all accounts, to be totally uninterested all through the trial. In spite of this fact, at a certain point, he communicated to his lawyer that he had a longing to live since God still had work for him to do.

Dempsey placed some of Fish's youngsters on the stand to testify for his peculiar conduct - self-whipping and sticking needles into his body, and in addition, his religious dreams. They likewise affirmed that he was a decent father who dependably accommodated them and never physically mistreated them.

Subsequent to being sentenced, Fish admitted the murder of the 8-year-old Francis X. McDonnell, murdered in Staten Island. At that time, Francis was playing in the entryway of his home, close to Port Richmond in Staten Island, on July 15, 1924. Francis's mother saw the old man strolling by, gripping and clenching his hands. He strolled past without saying a word. Later on in the day, that old man was seen once more. This time Fish was looking for Francis and his companions as they were playing. Francis's corpse was discovered in the forested areas where a nearby neighbor had chanced to see Francis and the man that evening. He had been ambushed and choked with his suspenders.

Fish arrived at the prison in March 1935

and was killed on January 16, 1936, by use of the electric chair in Sing Sing. Fish entered the chamber at around 11:06 p.m. and was pronounced dead three minutes later. He was buried in Sing Sing Prison's cemetery. A moment before the power switch was flipped, Fish expressed that he didn't know why he was there. It is said that his death took longer because of the various needles embedded into his privates that disrupted the power flow.

Days after the fact, a man from Staten Island approached to say he recognized Fish as the man who had attempted to bait his then eight-year-old little girl into the forested areas, some little distance from where Francis O'Donnell was killed three days later in 1924. The young lady, in her late high school years, saw him in his cell and remembered him. The "Gray Man" was found.

Fish was additionally connected to the 1932 murder of a fifteen-year-old girl named Mary O'Connor in Far Rockaway. The girl's battered corpse was found in the woods near a house which Fish had recently painted.

With those allegations from various provinces, there was no chance that Albert Fish would have been vindicated. His lone chance to avoid capital punishment was to have the alienists or therapists pronounce him legally insane.

More than fifty fingers, legs and other bones were found near the house where Albert Fish murdered Grace Budd.

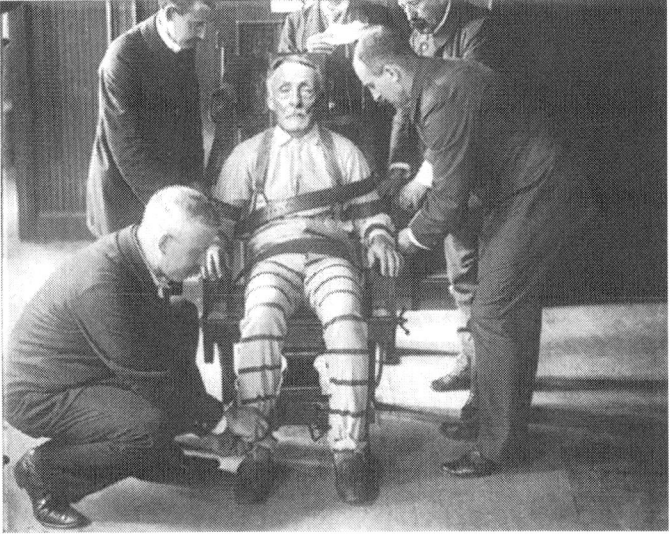

Execution

Chapter 2: Ted Bundy

"We serial killers are your sons, we are your husbands, we are everywhere. And there will be more of your children dead tomorrow" - Ted Bundy

Bundy represents himself in court.

Theodore Robert Bundy was born on November 24, 1946, at the Elizabeth Lund Home for Unwed Mothers. Later he was called Ted Bundy. He was an American killer who was involved in the murder of many young women. He committed his crimes all through the United States between the years 1974 and 1978. Ted escaped from prison two times and he was finally caught in February 1978. Although Ted constantly denied his murders for more than one decade, later on he confessed that he had committed 30 murders. However, the total number of the victims is unknown. The general estimate was around 35 murders, though the range was thought to be between 30 and over 100 murders. At first Ted performed his murders by bludgeoning his victims, and later he would strangle his victims to death. Ted was also involved in both rape and necrophilia, but he was mostly known as a rapist. He was later executed on January 24, 1989, in Florida through electrocution.

***

Bundy's mother was known as Louise Cowell, but facts about his father still remain a mystery. His mother could only say that she was seduced by a war soldier named Jack Worthington. Family members, however, expressed concern about Samuel Cowell being Ted's father and, as a consequence, he became violent. To avoid the stigma, his grandparents, Eleanor and Samuel Cowell, raised him as their own son. Therefore, Ted took their last name,

Cowell, and the boy grew up believing that his own mother was his sister. His biographers later accounted that, in the end, Ted discovered that Louise was his mother during his high school years. This was around 1969 after Bundy broke up with his girlfriend, according to Ann Rule, a true crime writer.

Bundy's mother lived in Philadelphia in his first years. Later, in 1950, Bundy's mother, whom he thought she was his elder sister, took the child and went to live with her relatives in Tacoma, Washington. This is where he had his surname altered to Nelson from Cowell. A year after moving away, Louise met John Culpepper Bundy at a singles night at the First Methodist Church in Tacoma. The couple married and later Bundy adopted Ted.

The couple had more kids, and Ted Bundy spent most of his time babysitting. Ted remained reserved about his stepfather, despite the fact that the man tried going on camping trips together or doing other father-son activities. Ted was considered a good scholar at Woodrow Wilson Secondary School in Tacoma, and he was an active member of the Methodist church. He also served as a vice-president of the Methodist Youth Fellowship. Moreover, he was involved in the Boy Scouts of America.

Bundy was shy and introverted all through high school and his initial years of college. He said that he was not able to comprehend social behaviors and this hindered his relational and social development. He also never understood how people get along and what make individuals want to become friends. He said he never knew what made people attractive to one another and he never comprehended what social interactions involved.

While in Florida, he remembered that he had had a fascination with violence as well as images of sex. During his prison interview, he called this part of himself 'the entity'. Bundy used to read material such as detective magazines and crime books. He mostly focused on materials that featured images of dead bodies or those that showed sexual violence. Before he left high school, Ted had been a compulsive robber and shoplifter, on the path to becoming a bandit. Due to his love for skiing, he stole skis as well as equipment and then faked ski-lift tickets. Bundy was captured two times as a juvenile wrongdoer; however, the records were later expunged.

After graduating from high school, Bundy received a scholarship to the University of Puget Sound. He took a course in Oriental studies as well as psychology. After one semester, Bundy decided to switch to Seattle University in Washington (UW). While still in college, Ted worked as a shelf stocker and a grocery bagger at the Safeway store located on Queen Anne Hill. Bundy also did other odd jobs. He later worked a night shift as an unpaid assistant at Seattle's Suicide Hot Line. This was a suicide prevention center which served the Seattle metropolitan and suburban areas. Bundy met a policewoman from Seattle, and they worked there together. She was known as Ann Rule, who wrote Bundy's crime biography.

He started a friendship with his fellow college student "Stephanie Brooks". He met her when he got into UW in 1967. After her 1968 graduation, she went back to her family's home in California after she had broken off the relationship. She was tired of what she perceived as Bundy's lack of ambition. That was when Ted chose to visit his birth place, Burlington, Vermont. There, as indicated by Rule, he went to the neighborhood records agent and discovered the reality of his parentage.

Prior to this revelation, Bundy had become a more confident individual. During 1968, he was able to manage the Seattle office of Nelson Rockefeller during the Presidential campaign, and he took part in the Republican convention hosted in Miami in 1968 as a Rockefeller booster. He re-enlisted at UW, now with an interest in psychology. Bundy was an honor student and was looked on favorably by his teachers. In 1969, he began seeing Elizabeth Kloepfer, who was a divorced secretary with a young daughter. She fell head over heels in love with him. They dated for over six years, and their affair lasted until he went to jail for kidnapping in 1976.

Ted Bundy graduated from UW in 1972 with a degree in psychology. Before long, he accepted a position in the Republican Party that included a warm friendship with Governor Daniel J. Evans. Amid the campaign, Bundy pursued Evans's democratic rival around the state, taping his speeches and reporting to Evans personally. A minor scandal started later when the Democrats learned about Ted, who had been pretending to be a college student.

During 1973, Ted enlisted in graduate school at the University of Utah. However, he wasn't serious and he started skipping classes, in the end withdrawing in 1974.

He was on a business trek to California during the mid-year of 1973. Bundy returned to his ex "Stephanie Brooks'" with another look and state of mind as he was more committed than before. Bundy kept on dating Kloepfer too, and neither of the women knew about the existence of the other. Ted sought Brooks all through the rest of the year, and she accepted his proposal to become engaged. After two weeks, soon after New Year's Eve of 1974, Bundy dumped her, declining to respond to telephone calls. A couple of weeks after this separation, Bundy started a deadly frenzy in Washington.

***

Nobody knows precisely when and where Bundy started killing. Numerous Bundy specialists, including Rule and ex-King County analyst Robert D. Keppel, say that Bundy may have begun murdering during his initial high school years. Ann Marie Burr was an 8-year-old girl from Tacoma who disappeared from her residence in 1961 when Ted was only 14 years of age. However, Bundy consistently stated he never killed her. The day preceding his execution, Ted told his legal advisor that he first attempted to abduct a woman in 1969 and hinted that he performed his first actual murder at some point in 1972. While confessing to Keppel, Ted said he committed his initial killing in 1972.

In 1973, one of Ted's Republican friends saw a set of handcuffs in the back of his Volkswagen. For a period of time, Bundy was a suspect in the December 1973 killing of Kathy

Devine from Washington State, yet DNA evidence suggested another man was responsible for that crime and he was incarcerated in 2002. Ted's most widely known and recognized killings were committed in 1974 when he was age 27.

Soon after 12 pm on January 4, 1974, Ted Bundy got into the basement room of 18-year-old Joni Lenz, an artist and a student from UW. Ted pummeled her using a metal piece from her bed while she was asleep and then sexually attacked her using a speculum. The victim was found by her apartment mates the following morning in a state of unconsciousness and lying in her own blood. She managed to survive the assault, yet she endured permanent brain injury.

Bundy's next victim was Lynda Ann Healey, another UW student. During morning time of February 1, 1974, Ted Bundy broke into her room, knocked her out, dressed her in pants and a shirt, and then wrapped her in a sheet and carried her away.

Co-eds started vanishing at a rate of around one a month. On March 12, 1974, at Olympia, Washington, Bundy abducted and killed Donna Gail Manson, a 19-year-old who was a student at Evergreen State College.

On April 17, 1974, Susan Rancourt

vanished from the Central Washington College. Two separate CWSC co-eds described seeing a man a few nights prior who was asking for help getting a stack of books to a Volkswagen.

Kathy Parks was the next one, and she vanished from the grounds of Oregon University. Brenda Ball was never seen again after leaving Flame Tavern on June 1, 1974. Ted then killed Georgann Hawkins, a student at UW and a member of the Kappa Alpha Theta sorority. Early on June 11th of 1974, she was traversing along a back street from her boyfriend's quarters to her sorority house. That was the last time she was seen. Witnesses talked of seeing Ted attempting to carry an attache case with his leg in a cast that night. One co-ed said the man had requested her assistance in carrying the bag to his auto, a Beetle.

Ted Bundy's Washington murder spree started on July 14, 1974, with the snatching of Denise Naslund and Janice Ott from Lake Sammamish State Park in Issaquah. On that day, eight separate individuals informed the police about an attractive young fellow with an injured arm who went by the name of "Ted". Five of them said that "Ted" requested their help in taking a sailboat off his car. One of them ran with "Ted" to his auto, saw that there wasn't any sailboat, then declined to go with him any closer. Three more witnesses confirmed seeing him with Ott, with this same tale about the sailboat and seeing her leave the shore area in his company. That was the last time she was seen alive. A few hours later, Naslund also vanished without a trace.

Detectives in King County now had a description of the suspect and his car. Several witnesses told the detectives that "Ted" talked with a clipped British accent. Before long, fliers were seen everywhere throughout the Seattle area. Subsequent to seeing the police sketch of the Lake Sammamish suspect in the daily papers and the TV news reports, Ted's girlfriend as well as a teacher at UW and his previous associate Ann Rule reported his name to police as a possibility. The police, receiving up to 200 tips each day, did not give due consideration to a tip concerning the well-groomed law student.

The remains of Naslund and Ott were found on September 7, 1974, off Interstate 90, just a mile away from the lakeside park. Alongside the victims were an additional vertebrae and femur bone that Ted later would verify as belonging to Georgann Hawkins, just before his execution.

From March to March 3, 1975, jawbones

and skulls were found on Taylor Mountain east of Issaquah. It was determined that they belonged to murder victims Parks, Healy, Rancourt, and Ball. Bundy later insisted that he had dumped Donna Manson's corpse there as well. However, there was no trace of her.

Bundy flashed smiles at the cameras while contending he was blameless at a press conference when he was arraigned on first-degree murder charges.

When Bundy began attending Utah University graduate school in Salt Lake City, he continued killing. On October 2, 1974, Nancy Wilcox vanished from Holladay, Utah. Wilcox was last spotted riding in a Volkswagen.

On October 18, 1974, Ted Bundy raped, sodomized, and strangled Melissa Smith, the 17-year-old daughter of Midvale police chief, Louis Smith. Her body was discovered on October 11th. On October 31, Laura Aime, also 17, vanished following a Halloween party in Lehi, Utah. Almost a month later, her nude body was discovered by hikers in a stream in Fork Canyon. She had been beaten and strangled.

In Murray, on November 8, 1974, Carol DaRonch barely got away with her life. Posing as Officer Roseland of the Murray Police

Department, Ted Bundy approached her at the Fashion Place Mall and told her that somebody had attempted to break into her car. He insisted that she go with him to the police station. She got into his auto but she did not fasten her safety belt. They drove for a brief period before Bundy abruptly pulled over to the shoulder and slapped handcuffs on her. During the confusion of battle, he attached both cuffs to the same wrist. Ted grabbed a crowbar, but DaRonch managed to grab the crowbar just before having her skull broken. Then she opened the car door and tumbled to the expressway, getting away from her intended murderer.

Around an hour later, an unknown man appeared at Viewmont School in Bountiful located in Utah, where the drama club was performing a play. He approached a teacher and a student, asking them both to accompany him to the parking area to identify a car. They both refused. The teacher saw him again just before the play ended. Ted Bundy now was breathing hard, his hair was disarranged, and his shirt was untucked. One more student had seen the man hiding at the back of the amphitheater. Debby Kent was a 17-year-old girl from Viewmont High who had left the play to go and get her brother. She was not seen again. Later, agents found a tiny key in the parking area outside Viewmont High School that opened the handcuffs of Carol DaRonch.

During 1975, while going to graduate school at the University of Utah, Ted moved his slaughter to Colorado. On January 12, 1975, Caryn Campbell vanished from Wildwood Inn in Snowmass, Colorado, where she on holiday with her fiance and his children. She vanished in the 50 feet between the elevators and her room. Her body was found more than a month later, on February 17, 1975.

On March 15, 1975, ski instructor Julie Cunningham vanished in Vail. On April 6, 1975, Denise Oliverson vanished in Grand Junction. While imprisoned, Bundy admitted to the Colorado authorities that he was using crutches when he asked Cunningham to help him carry the ski boots to the car. Near the car, Bundy clubbed her using a crowbar before handcuffing her. Reminiscent of the Hawkins murder, he later strangled her.

On May 6, 1975, Lynette Culver disappeared from her school in Pocatello, Idaho. Susan Curtis disappeared on June 28th, 1975, following Bundy's return to Utah. The corpses of Cunningham, Curtis, Culver, and Oliverson were never retrieved.

In the meantime, back in Washington, detectives were trying to organize their massive list of suspects. They utilized PCs to cross-check distinctive likely characteristics of suspects (colleagues of Lynda Healy, proprietors of Volkswagens, and so on) against each other, and after that identify, based on speculations, suspects who showed up on more than a single list. Theodore Robert Bundy was among 25 individuals who later turned up on four different lists. His find was second in line to be checked when a call from Utah informed them of Bundy's arrest.

***

Bundy was apprehended on August 16, 1975, in Salt Lake City because of his failure to stop for a policeman. A search of his car revealed a ski mask, a crowbar, handcuffs, garbage bags, an ice pick, and different things that were believed by police officers to be burglary tools. Bundy was calm while being questioned, stating that he used the mask for skiing and that he found the manacles in a dumpster. A Utah detective named Jerry Thompson associated Bundy with DaRonch's kidnapping as well as with the missing women, and he searched Bundy's residence.

The search turned up a leaflet of Colorado

ski resorts with a notation by Wildwood Inn, the place where Caryn Campbell was last seen alive. Bundy was then put in a lineup viewed by DaRonch and the other witnesses. DaRonch identified Bundy as "Officer Roseland" and other witnessed stated that he was hanging around the night that Debby Kent vanished.

On March 1, 1976, following a one-week trial, Ted was found guilty of DaRonch's abduction. He was sentenced to fifteen years in the Utah State Prison. The authorities in Colorado wanted Bundy for murder charges, and he was removed there for trial.

On June 7, 1977, as he was preparing for a court hearing in the Caryn Campbell trial, Ted was relocated to the Pitkin County Court in Aspen. During a court break, he was permitted to visit the law library. He leaped from a second story window and got away. However, he sprained his right leg in the process. After his escape, he first ran, then walked sedately through the little town toward Aspen Mountain.

Ted walked as far as the highest point of Aspen Mountain without being recognized. There Bundy rested for two days in a deserted hunting shelter. Yet, a while later, he became disoriented and couldn't tell east from west. He meandered around the mountain, missing two trails that would have brought him to his destination, Crested Butte. At a certain point, he encountered a local man with a gun who was among the ones looking for Bundy. However, he escaped being apprehended.

On June 13, 1977, Bundy stole an auto he discovered on the mountain. He was driving to Aspen and almost got away, but two policemen saw the Cadillac with darkened headlights weaving all over the road and they pulled Ted over. They realized who he was and transported him back to prison. Ted Bundy had been out for six days.

Bundy was back in jail, but he had another plan in mind. Bundy was being held in the jail at Glenwood Springs, Colorado, while he was awaiting his trial. He had obtained a blade from a hacksaw and $500 in cold cash. He later said that the blade was obtained from another jail prisoner. For more than two weeks, he sawed through the welds holding a little metal plate on the ceiling and, as he consumed fewer calories, he was able to fit through the opening and slither to the space above.

A witness in the jail said that he had heard Ted moving around above the ceiling during the evenings before his escape, yet no action was taken. On December 23, 1977, Ted Bundy's

Aspen judge established issued a ruling that Caryn Campbell's murder trial would begin on January 9th, 1978. He later changed the location to Colorado Springs. Bundy understood that he needed to escape prior to his being moved out of the Glenwood Springs jail.

On December 30, 1977, Ted dressed in warm clothes and stuffed books and records under his cover to give the appearance that he was asleep. Bundy wriggled through the opening and into the crawlspace. He crept to a spot specifically over the prison guard's storeroom - the corrections officer and his better half were out for the night - dropped into the corrections officer's residence and left through the door.

Bundy was free. However, he was walking during an icy Colorado night. He stole an MG, but it broke down in the mountains. Thus, Ted was stuck on Interstate 70 at night in a snowstorm. However, he was fortunate to find another driver who offered him a ride to Vail. From that point, he rode a bus to Denver and boarded for a flight to Chicago. In the Glenwood Springs jail, the jailors did not see that Bundy was missing until twelve noon on December 31, 1977, 17 hours after Bundy's escape, and Bundy was in Chicago by that time.

***

After landing in Chicago, Ted boarded an Amtrak to Ann Arbor, Michigan, where Bundy found lodging at the YMCA. On January 2, 1978, Ted headed to an Ann Arbor bar, where he watched the University of Washington play Michigan in the Rose Bowl. Bundy stole a car in Ann Arbor that he later abandoned in Atlanta, Georgia. There he caught a bus to Tallahassee, Florida, arriving on January 8, 1978. He rented a room at a motel under the pseudonym of "Chris Hagen", then he carried out some illegal activities including shoplifting, purse grabbing, and a car theft.

He stole an ID card of a student that shared a place with Kenneth Misner, and then he searched for duplicates of Misner's Social Security card and birth certificate. He now had a moustache and he drew a mole on his right cheek. Otherwise, Bundy made no real effort at disguising his identity. Bundy looked for a job at a construction site, yet when a staff member asked for his driver's license as a proof of identity, Bundy left. He did not look elsewhere for employment.

After Bundy arrived in Tallahassee, on Super Bowl Sunday, January 15, 1978, more than two years of suppressed violence exploded. Ted got to the Chi Omega house at Florida State

University at around 3 a.m. There he beat and strangled two sleeping students, Lisa Levy and Margaret Bowman. He also sexually violated Levy. He additionally beat two other Chi Omega women, Karen Chandler and Kathy Kleiner. The whole attack took about 30 minutes. Subsequent to leaving the sorority house, Bundy broke into a home at some distance away where he clubbed Cheryl Thomas, another Florida State University student.

On February 9, 1978, Ted ventured out to Lake City in Florida. There, he kidnapped, raped, and killed 12-year-old Kimberly Leach, tossing her body below a small pig shelter. On February 12, 1978, Ted stole another Volkswagen, then he left Tallahassee, travelling west over the Florida panhandle.

On February 15, 1978, not long past 1 a.m., Ted was stopped by Pensacola police officer David Lee. At the point when the officer checked the car license, the car showed up as stolen. Ted resisted the officer but he was overpowered. As Lee transported the suspect to prison, Bundy said that he wished they had killed him. Upon his retention, he gave the police his name as Ken Misner. However, the Florida Law Enforcement made a fingerprint match early the following day. He was promptly taken to Tallahassee and accused of the Tallahassee and the Lake City murders. Ted was later transferred to Miami for trial in the Chi Omega deaths.

***

According to William Hagmaier, Special Agent of the FBI Behavioral Sciences Unit, Bundy was convicted of murder in just a few days, paving the way to his execution. However, in the long run, he died. Around 7:06 a.m. on January 24, 1989, Bundy was killed in the electric chair at State Prison located in Starke, Florida. Ted's last words were that he would like to send his affection to his family and friends. More than 2,000 volts were conducted through his body for not more than two minutes. He was declared dead around 7:16 a.m. Several hundred individuals were assembled outside the jail and broke out in cheers when they saw the signal indicating that Ted had been proclaimed dead.

THE MANY FACES OF TED BUNDY

The many faces of Ted Bundy. He was a chameleon who rarely looked the same way twice.

Bundy possessed almost nondescript facial features and few distinguishing marks, and was able to drastically change his appearance with very little effort.

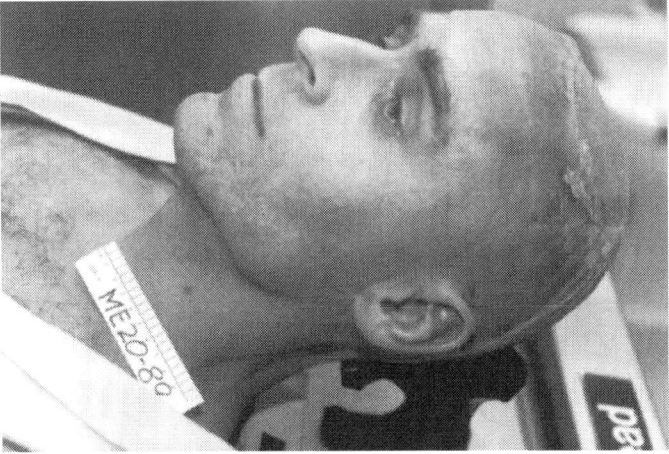

Ted Bundy after execution Jan. 24 1989

Chapter 3: Dennis Nilsen

"Being a loner has its advantages, a self-containment necessary for keeping body and 'soul' alive and progressing. Dying in prison is not such a great problem as living in prison." - Dennis Nilsen

Dennis Nilsen was born on November 23, 1945, in Fraserburgh, Scotland. He was called the Muswell Hill Murderer or the Kindly Killer, a serial killer who lived in London, England.

He murdered no less than fifteen men and young boys in ghastly circumstances between 1978 and 1983 and was known for keeping the bodies for further sex acts. In the end, however,

Nilsen was caught after he tried flushing the eviscerated human parts and clogged his drainage unit. The cleaning organization found that the channels were completely blocked by pieces of human flesh and called the police.

Because of the similarities between their sexuality, crimes, and way of life, Nilsen has been called the "English Jeffrey Dahmer".

***

Born on November 23, 1945, Dennis Nilsen was the child of Norwegian Olav Nilsen, a soldier, and Scottish Betty Whyte, who managed a very strict family in Fraserburgh, a fishing town in the center of Aberdeenshire, Scotland. Nilsen's father demonstrated little interest for his family, spending much of his life away from home, and finally abandoning them at the time Dennis was only six years old. At this point, Nilsen's first five years were the most joyful years of his entire life, he indicated, as he lived them with a great role model whom he adored more than any other person. This was his grandfather, Andrew Whyte.

He was a very strict man and proud. He objected to such things such as liquor, the radio and working on Sabbath days. He appeared to have a genuine satisfaction in the relationship with Nilsen. The two used to go walking for long periods, and Nilsen would listen to his granddad's stories about the ocean. Unavoidably, as with numerous relationships, Nilsen's structure in his life ended on Halloween, 1951. Whyte was discovered dead, lying in his fishing vessel. He was just 62 years of age.

Nilsen, being only six years old at that time, was never told that his granddad was dead. Instead, he was simply told that he was asleep. Nilsen saw his grandpa lying in the coffin. Nilsen himself contends that this was his most vivid memory from his childhood. No one realized how serious that early encounter with a dead corpse was going to be for him later in his life.

Nilsen was disappointed and traumatized when, after so many months, he understood his grandfather was never returning. It is clear that this mental pain thrust Nilsen into his universe of loneliness, and he could never again adore someone else wholeheartedly as he did his grandfather. It would be unfair to say he never had a normal childhood. He held affection for animals and he would care for them most of his life. Nilsen kept pigeons. He was heartbroken when a vandal killed them for no reason. Nilsen had likewise acquired a great connection with the ocean, thanks to his grandfather Whyte. Therefore, he used to spend a lot of hours along the ocean shore.

Nilsen was sexually uninitiated in school, in spite of feeling some longings on various occasions. At a certain point, he had become infatuated with the child of a nearby clergyman. Another object of fantasy was only a character in a French language book, Pierre Duvan. Nilsen's school results were not remarkable and he opted to join the army at the age of 15.

Nilsen's initial three years in army were mostly spent in training at the Depot located in Aldershot Barracks in Southern England. To him, this was an uncommonly happy time because he excelled with the diligent work and loved the comradeship of his army life. Nilsen now felt he belonged, but he sometimes felt an attraction to various comrades.

Nilsen harbored feelings of guilt, but he consoled himself with the thought that he was likely bisexual. Nilsen had to pick a trade in the army and he chose to cook; he also learned the skills involved in butchery, a skill he would use later. Nilsen delighted in the camaraderie, and he was well-liked by the other officers, but unfortunately he was also familiarized with the use of strong liquor.

At that time, he had numerous sexual

contacts with men, as well as with a Bavarian prostitute and a youthful Arab boy. It was while he was still serving in the Middle East that Nilsen started to have a disturbing interest in viewing himself as a dead man. Nilsen would cover his whole body with powder, blue his lips, then masturbate while gazing at his image in the mirror. Love and dying had started to blend in his mind.

Later towards the end of this period, Nilsen, who had achieved the rank of a Corporal, was sent to the Shetland Islands where he fell in love with an 18-year-old private. Unrequited affections caused Nilsen to keep his feelings hidden. He was dismayed because his love was never returned. It was during his very last night in Shetland that Nilsen burned several movies that they had made together. Many of his colleagues were shocked by his actions. Altogether, Nilsen's army career lasted for 11 years and 3 months.

Sometime later, Nilsen became disenchanted with the Army's actions in Northern Ireland. Nilsen left the army with bitterness due to the political issues of the time. Upon his release from service, he returned to Fraserburgh and spent around five weeks with the family he grew up with. Nilsen's mother Betty had remarried and she now lived with her second spouse, Adam Scott. Nilsen had arguments with his sibling over the topic of homosexuality. Their disagreement was so severe that the siblings never again spoke to each other.

In December 1972, Nilsen enlisted in the Metropolitan Police, hoping to find the camaraderie that he had felt in the army. Nilsen was given the number Q287, but he found little comradeship among the police. He often visited the gay bars in London, such as the King William IV, Colerne, the Golden Lion, and the Black Cap.

***

All of his victims were either students or homeless people whom he picked up in bars and brought home either for sex or only for company. Nilsen strangled or drowned his victims during the night, awakening with no memory of the things he had done. He learned how to butcher while in the army, and this was helpful in discarding the bodies. Nilsen had access to an extensive garden where he could burn some of the remains in a fire.

In 1981, he moved to the upstairs apartment. This made it difficult to get rid of the body parts. He had bags brimming with human organs in his closet, and plastic sacks with human remains under the floorboards. Neighbors complained about the smell. When he attempted to flush the pieces down in the latrine, he clogged the sewer system of his home in Muswell Hill, north London. At the point when a team was called to unblock the drain, they first observed the drain was stuffed with a fleshy substance. The investigator then called his director to check it out.

On the following day, the drain was finally cleared. However, the drain investigator and his director were suspicious and called the police. After a closer examination, some little bones and what looked like chicken meat were discovered inside a pipe that originated from Nilson's drain. They were later found to be human.

Dennis Nilsen was apprehended in 1983 as a suspect in several deaths. Nilsen apologized to the policemen for not being able to tell them the number of individuals he had killed. At the point when his home was checked, three heads were discovered in a pantry. They also discovered 13 more bodies at Nilsen's previous address in Crinkleroot, Melrose Avenue.

During the trials at Old Bailey, he was cold and aloof and appeared to be totally unaffected by the fact that he had killed 15 individuals. Nilsen was sentenced by the judge to life in prison with a minimum term of 25 years. Then the Home Secretary ordered an entire life sentence, which implied he could never be discharged. In any case, after the Home Secretary was stripped of the authority to set terms in November of 2002, the result was that Nilsen could be released on life permit in 2008 because of the 25-year minimum. In 1993 he was given authorization to give a televised interview from the prison.

First murder: Nilsen's first murder occurred on December 30, 1978. Nilsen recounted that he had encountered his first victim in a gay bar. He choked him with a necktie until he lost consciousness and then drowned him in a bucket of water. On January 12, 2006, it was determined that the victim was Stephen Holmes, who was born on March 22, 1964, and was thus only 14 years old at the time of his death. Holmes was on his way home, returning from a musical concert.

Between the first and the second murders, he tried to kill a student from Hong Kong that he met in West End. Nilsen was questioned by the police, but the student chose not to prosecute him, and Nilsen was not charged with a crime.

Second Murder: The second victim was a Canadian student known as Kenneth Ockendon. Nilsen strangled him during their sexual activity.

Unlike many other victims, Ockendon was reported as a missing person.

Third Murder: Martyn Duffy was a 16-year-old homeless boy from Birkenhead. In May 1980, Nilsen invited Duffy to come home with him. The boy was strangled and then drowned in the kitchen sink.

Fourth Murder: Billy Sutherland was known to be a male prostitute originating from Scotland. Nilsen couldn't recall how he killed Sutherland. Nonetheless, it was later reported that the victim had been manually strangled.

Fifth Murder: The fifth victim was another male prostitute who was never identified. All that is known is that he was most likely from Thailand or the Philippines.

Sixth Murder: Nilsen could recall little about this victim as well as the next two victims. All that Nilsen could remember about victim number six was that he was a young Irish laborer that he had encountered in a bar.

Seventh Murder: Nilsen described the seventh victim as a down-and-out "hippie-type" whom Nilsen had discovered sleeping in an doorway in the Charing Cross area.

Eighth Murder: Nilsen could remember nothing about his eighth victim.

Ninth and Tenth Murders: Both victims were young Scotsmen whom he encountered in bars in Soho.

Eleventh Murder: The eleventh victim was a skinhead Nilsen met at Piccadilly Circus who had a tattoo circling his neck that read "cut here". The man had bragged to Nilsen about how tough he was and how much he enjoyed fighting. In any case, once he was totally drunk, he proved to be no match for the killer Nilsen, who hung his nude torso in his room for 24 hours before he was deposited under the floorboards.

At some point between victims 6 and 11, on November 10, 1980, a potential victim of Nilsen woke up as he was being choked and managed to fight off his aggressor. Despite calling the policemen very quickly after the assault, the officers took no action because they considered it to be a domestic argument between two gay lovers.

Twelfth Murder: The twelfth victim was a man named Malcolm Barlow. On September 18, 1981 Nilsen discovered him in a doorway near his home. He took him in, and then he called an emergency vehicle for him. Barlow was discharged from the hospital the following day and came back to Nilsen's home to express his gratitude toward him. He was delighted to be invited for a supper and a couple of drinks. He was killed that night.

Nilsen encountered a drag queen in a bar in Camden. After being strangled, he regained consciousness as Nilsen was attempting to drown him in an icy bath and was able to fight him off.

Thirteenth Murder: John Howlett was the first to be killed in Nilsen's new home in December of 1981. He was one of only a few who managed to fight back. In any case, Nilsen now despised him and was resolved that he had to die. During a strenuous fight, Howlett attempted to choke Nilsen. However, Howlett was drowned after having his head submerged in water for five minutes. Howlett's corpse was the first to be dismembered in the attic flat. Then the different body parts were either stashed around the house or flushed down the latrine.

Fourteenth Murder: The next victim was Graham Allen, another homeless man who met Nilsen in Shaftesbury Avenue. After killing him, he left his body in the bathroom, not sure what to do with it. Three days later, Graham was also dismembered just like Nilsen's previous victim.

Fifteenth Murder: Nilsen's last victim was a drug addict known as Stephen Sinclair. On February 1, 1983, Nilsen met him in Oxford

Street and invited him to go to his place. After indulging in liquor and heroin, Sinclair was strangled and his body was cut up. It was pieces of Sinclair's remains that blocked the drains of Nilsen's home and initially brought Nilsen's murders to the attention of the police.

***

Many women and men had visited Nilsen and hadn't been hurt. Some of them who managed to escape being murdered reported the case to the police. Had this led to more thorough investigations, it might have in turn saved quite a number of lives. Nilsen dumped a lot of bodies in the drains and into the rear garden. A man once found a plastic bag that had pieces which looked like ribs and a spinal column. The man never reported the case so this discovery was never tied to Nilsen's murders.

In the apartment where he was living, there were five other tenants. None of them knew Nilsen very well. In early February, one tenant realized that one of the toilets was not flushing. The tenant attempted to clear the blockage using acid, but it was not successful. Another toilet also had the same problems. In this instance, a plumber came to look into the matter, but his tools were ineffective, so he called specialists. Nilsen now feared that all he had been doing was about to come to light. So he took all the remaining parts of his victim and locked them in a closet and ceased flushing the toilet.

After two days, the company assigned the drain work to Dyno-Rod. Michael Cattran began analyzing the drain and he suggested that the problem was in the underground. So Cattran went in the main hole to check it out. He noticed a strange smell, like something dead. He saw some sludge that was about 8 inches wide on the sewer's floor. Then he realized that the sludge was made up of between 30 to 40 pieces of flesh. The sludge had come from the pipe that led to the house. When reporting his findings to his superiors, the tenants, including Nilsen, gathered around him as he made the call, and Cattran felt that they should call the police. His company would, however, do a better analysis during the day. The technician took Nilsen to the other side of the house to see the rotten flesh. Later that night, Nilsen went back and removed all the flesh particles and threw them away over the fence. He even thought to replace the pieces with chicken parts. He again contemplated suicide, but instead he stayed there alone with the remains of three bodies surrounding him.

Some of the downstairs tenants had taken notice of his movements. When Cattran returned and found that the drain was cleared, they told him about their suspicion. Cattran pulled a foul-smelling chunk of meat from the sewer and then called the police. The following day at his workplace, Nilsen told a co-worker that if he wasn't at work the next day, it was because he would either be sick, in jail or dead. The co-worker just laughed. Nilsen, however, sensed that something was coming down. When he entered his house to go up to his apartment, he saw three men there waiting for him.

Detective Jay told Nilsen that the reason they were there was that some human remains had blocked the sewer. In dismay, Nilsen asked where they had come from. They told him it was from his apartment and asked him to turn over the rest of the corpse. At that point, Nilsen gave himself up and said that he would accompany them to the police station. He admitted he knew his rights and wanted to talk. He talked at length and as he talked, the police realized that they had received clues, and had they reacted differently, they could have stopped the killer and saved lives.

Upon a further search of his apartment revealed several bags of male body parts. These parts were taken to the mortuary for investigation. Nilsen advised them to check under a drawer in the bathroom and to look in the tea chest. He pointed out the other apartment where he had previously lived. There, he said, he had killed 11 or 13 men.

***

Nilsen's formal interrogation began on February 11th and lasted for 30 hours, all being spread out over the week. He discussed the techniques he used and later assisted the police to identify the parts of the murdered victims. He had all the information in his mind, and it flowed out as if he wanted to get rid of every memory. He showed no remorse, nor displayed any digressions. He revealed that his professional training had allowed him to fake calmness. He provided the police with the information that they needed to ensure his conviction.

He helped the police to gather the pieces and put them together to identify the victims. This caused them to charge Nilsen and hold him until further investigation. Later on, Nilsen led the police to Melrose Avenue where he had buried the other parts and made bonfires.

After his confessions, Nilsen was removed to Brixton Prison to await his trial. He was dismayed by the reactions of the press following his arrest.

In October 1979, a man named Andrew made a complaint that Nilsen had attacked him. He never agreed to write a statement or to attend court as a witness. There was no follow-up on this case. A year later, another man named Douglas Stewart also said that Nilsen attacked him while he was asleep in the armchair. He knocked Nilsen down and then Nilsen told him to leave. At around 4 a.m., he called the police who noticed that he had been drinking. Upon knocking on Nilsen's door, they figured out that it was a homosexual conflict. However, they made a report even though Stewart failed to follow up.

In his Carney garden, Nilsen lived for more than one year and killed more men. On November 23, 1981, it was his 36th birthday and he took a 19-year-old gay student named Paul Nobbs home with him for drinks. They went to bed and Paul woke around 2 a.m. with a bad headache. He got up at six and went to the kitchen. He saw a red mark on his neck and his face seemed bruised. Nilsen told him that he looked bad and he should see a doctor. Upon the doctor's examination, he found out that someone had tried to strangle Nobbs. He, however, failed to report the case for fear of exposing his own lifestyle. After Nobbs, there was yet another victim who escaped.

On New Year's Eve, friends and neighbors were invited to Nilsen's apartment. They were uneasy because Nilsen seemed drunk. Later, they heard him returning home with someone. Then the neighbors heard noises upstairs. A man came running and told them that he had already told the police that Nilsen tried to murder him. The case was not pursued.

Another victim who escaped Nilsen's murder was Carl Stotter who woke up unable to breathe. He thought Nilsen was helping him. Nilsen took him to the bathtub and attempted to drown him, and Stotter begged him to stop. He lost consciousness and Nilsen thought he was dead, so he carried him to the couch. Upon realizing he was not dead, he took him to bed and wrapped himself around him. After Stotter regained consciousness, Nilsen told him some lies about what happened. After a checkup, he realized that his condition resulted from strangulation, but he never reported the incident.

***

Nilsen wrote over fifty notebooks to help him regain his memory for his prosecution. He was charged with six counts of killings and two attempted murders. The prosecutor Alan Green affirmed that Nilsen had done the killings while being fully aware. The defense only relied on psychiatric analysis. Nilsen claimed not guilty for all the charges laid against him.

Nilsen attempted to undermine the credibility of those who testified against him by assisting the lawyers in pointing out errors with some of their statements. The interviews which Nilsen had with the police were read for four hours. Some of the evidence that was presented in the court were a cooking pot, a cutting board and knives.

The defense witness, Dr. James McKeith, talked about the various aspects of an unspecified personality disorder that he believed Nilsen suffered from. He pointed out how Nilsen always had a hard time expressing his feelings. He always fled from relationships that had gone wrong. The psychiatrist also connected Nilsen's sexual arousal with the unconscious bodies. He termed him as narcissistic which added to his amnesia due to too much drinking.

Another psychiatrist named Dr. Paul Bowden who spent 14 hours with Nilsen for this case termed Nilsen's condition a mental abnormality but not a mental disorder. This had the effect of confusing the jury. During the conclusion of the case, the jury was instructed by the judge that a person's mind can be evil without being abnormal. This assurance cleared up the psychiatric jargon.

The jury retired on November 3rd, and the following day at around 11 a.m. the judge said that he would accept a majority count. This was because there were two dissenters on each issue apart from the murder of Nobbs. They later delivered a ruling saying that Nilsen was guilty on all counts.

The judge sentenced Nilsen to life imprisonment. He would not be eligible for parole for 25 years. Nilsen was then 38 years old.

Nilsen became a featured character who had a huge influence on many fictional writers. The one that represents most of his killing is known as Exquisite Corpse invented by Poppy Brite. Like Nilsen's, his casualties were homeless people, and he would deal with them so as to make them malleable. The same as Nilsen did, he delighted in the act of murder, yet he didn't much like the dissection that followed.

He kept them beside him for as long as a week, and he was not mindful of the smell of death. He needed them with him so he would not feel alone. As he cut them up, he drank liquor, much the same as Nilsen, and after he was detained, he filled various notepads with his contemplation and memories. In spite of the fact that Andrew Compton in Exquisite Corpse is even more of a predator than Nilsen, his psychology is derived from his real-life counterpart.

Chapter 4: Jeffrey Dahmer

"The killing was a means to an end. That was the least satisfactory part. I didn't enjoy doing that. That's why I tried to create living zombies with uric acid in the drill [to the head], but it never worked. No, the killing was not the objective. I just wanted to have the person under my complete control, not having to consider their wishes, being able to keep them there as long as I wanted." - Jeffrey Dahmer

Jeffrey Dahmer is one of the most well-known serial killers in the world. He is said to have killed 17 men and boys. It seems that most of his killing was around the Milwaukee area during

1978 and 1991. The man was responsible for the death, rape, and dismemberment of boys and men. Due to his monstrous crimes he committed, Jeffrey Dahmer was nicknamed the 'Milwaukee Cannibal'. His murders also involved necrophilia and preservation of some parts of the body, as well as cannibalism.

***

Dahmer was born in West Allis, Wisconsin, to Joyce Annette and Lionel Dahmer. His father was an analytical scientific expert. Seven years after his birth, his sibling David was born. Joyce Dahmer, his mother, allegedly had a troublesome pregnancy with her older son. When Jeffrey was eight years old, he and his family moved to Bath, Ohio,.

Dahmer became progressively reserved and uncommunicative between the ages of 10 and 15. He indicated little enthusiasm for any social activities or hobbies. He cycled round the surrounding environment searching for dead creatures that he later dismembered in the forested areas close to his home or even at home.

In one occasion, he placed a puppy's head onto a stake. Despite the fact that he was an outcast in the Revere High School, he got to be something of a cult idol among a few students because of his imitation of his mother's interior decorator who suffered cerebral palsy. At some point during his adolescence, Dahmer started drinking, and he was a drunkard by the time he graduated from secondary school.

His parents, Lionel Herbert and Joyce Dahmer divorced during his teen years. Dahmer went to the Ohio State University, but he left after the first quarter, due to the fact that he neglected to go to his classes. Dahmer was drunk for most of the school term, so his father compelled him to enlist in the Army. He excelled at the beginning of his tour of duty. However, he was discharged from military duty after two years as a result of his liquor addiction.

In 1981, the year when the Army released Dahmer, he was offered a plane ticket to any place in the nation. Dahmer told the police that he couldn't head home to live with his father. Instead, he chose to go to Miami Beach, Florida. The reason behind this choice was that he was weary of being cold. He liked to hang out at a medical facility, but he was later tossed out for drinking. Although he came back home, he kept on drinking a great deal, and he was arrested for disorderly conduct and drinking.

In 1982, Dahmer moved in with his grandmother in West Allis and stayed there for six years. During this time, his conduct became progressively peculiar. His grandmother found a fully clad male mannequin in his room. It turned out that Dahmer had filched it from a certain store. Another event was that she found a .357 Magnum beneath Dahmer's bed. What is more, horrible odors originated from the house basement. He said to his father that he had come home with a dead squirrel and disintegrated it using some chemicals. Dahmer was apprehended two times for indecent exposure, both in 1982 and 1986. His second offense involved masturbating in the presence of two young children.

During the summer of 1988, Dahmer's grandmother asked him to move out due to his late evenings, his odd conduct, and the foul scents originating from the underground room. He later found a condo in Milwaukee on the West side. The place was near to his employment at Ambrosia Chocolate Company.

On September 26, 1988, a day after moving into his newly acquired apartment, he was captured for sedating and sexually stroking a boy of 13 in Milwaukee. This led to him being sentenced to five years' probation and one year in a work release camp. Dahmer was ordered to register as a sex offender. He was paroled from the work release camp two months early and he again moved into a new apartment. Thereafter, he started a series of murders that led to his capture in 1991.

***

Dahmer confessed his very initial murder took place in mid-year of 1978 when he was 18 years old. His father was away on a business trip and his mother had moved out taking Dahmer's sibling with her. So Dahmer was left alone. In June, Dahmer encountered a hitchhiker named Stephen Hicks and invited him to his father's home to drink beer. Dahmer was planning to engage in a sexual relationship with him.

When Hicks attempted to leave, Dahmer clubbed Hicks to death by hitting his head with a 10-pound dumbbell. Dahmer later said that he had committed the crime because the person intended to leave and he wanted him to stay. Dahmer interred the dead body in the yard. Nine years went by before he murdered someone else. In 1987, in the month of September, Dahmer picked up 26-year-old Steven Tuomi from a bar, then he murdered him on an impulse. Later he contended he had no remembrance of committing that crime.

After that murder, he kept on killing

sporadically. He committed two additional murders in 1988 and one more in 1989. More often he encountered his victims in gay bars and engaged in sexual relations with them before slaying them. He preserved the skull of one victim, Anthony Sears, until he was apprehended.

In May 1990, Dahmer got out of his grandmother's home and into Apartment 213 at 924 North 25th Street in Milwaukee. Dahmer committed four more murders in the latter part of the year 1990 and two more murders in February, one in April 1991 and yet another in May 1991.

On May 27th, 1991, during the morning hours, Konerak Sinthasomphone, the younger brother of the boy whom Dahmer had assaulted in 1988, was found in the city, walking around naked, badly affected by drugs and bleeding from his rectum. Two ladies from the area found the disoriented boy and called 911. Dahmer caught up with his victim and attempted to take him back, but the ladies managed to stop him. John Balcerzak, a police officer, and his partner Josephn Gabrish, who were sent to the location were told by Dahmer that Sinthasomphone was his boyfriend and that he was 19 years old. He said that they had quarrelled while drinking. This was despite the protests of the two ladies that had phoned 911. They said they remembered the boy from the area and said he was a youngster who couldn't communicate in English. Regardless, the officers gave him to Dahmer.

The officers detected a bad smell was coming from Dahmer's apartment, but they did not look into it. The bad odor was coming from Tony Hughes's body, Dahmer's past victim, who was decomposing in another room. The officers never made any endeavor to confirm Sinthasomphone's personality or age, nor find somebody who could speak with him, and they neglected to run a background check that would have exposed Dahmer as a registered sex offender who was under probation. Before the night was over, Dahmer had murdered and dissected Sinthasomphone, preserving his skull.

During the summer of 1991, Dahmer was killing at a rate of one person every week. He executed Matt Turner on 30th June. He then killed Jeremiah Weinberger on 5th July, and on July 12th he killed Oliver Lacy. Lastly, on July 19th, he murdered Joseph Brandehoft.

Dahmer dreamt of being able to transform his victims into "zombies" — totally compliant, endlessly energetic sex slaves. He endeavored to do so by drilling holes in the victims' skulls and introducing hydrochloric acid or boiling water to the frontal lobe of their brains with a syringe while the victim was still alive. Other tenants in the Oxford Apartments smelt terrible odors originating from Apartment 213, as well as the thumps of falling things and the intermittent humming of a power saw. Unlike many other serial killers, Dahmer murdered people belonging to a variety of races.

His custom for tracking, killing and discarding his victims was generally the same. He welcomed his victims to his apartment to watch sexually-explicit films or to pose for photographs. He used tranquilizers and later gave them drink. When the victims were drunk, Dahmer choked them with his hands or using a strap. Every now and again, he engaged in sexual relations with the carcass and later he dismembered them.

Prior to any tidy up, Dahmer used to get out his Polaroid to immortalize the whole experience so he could recall every single murder. At that point, he cut into their torsos, and he was fascinated by the shade of their insides and excited by the warmth that the freshly murdered body was emitting. At last, he would dissect the man, capturing every phase of the procedure for his future pleasure.

He discarded a large portion of the bodies, testing different methods with different acids and chemicals that would destroy the flesh. A few sections of the remains he kept as trophies, regularly the sex organs and the head. The genitals were preserved in formaldehyde. The victims' heads were boiled until the tissue fell off. When the skull was stripped clean, he colored it with dark paint to resemble plastic.

***

Dahmer lured another man named Tracy Edwards on July 22, 1991. Dahmer tussled with Edwards so as to restrain him, but he neglected to tie his wrists together. Using a huge butcher knife, Dahmer coerced Edwards into the room. Edwards saw photos of ravaged bodies on the walls and smelled the ghastly scent originating from a huge blue barrel that was filled with powerful corrosive which broke down human bodies into ooze for disposal through the latrine. Edwards punched him in the face, then kicked him in the stomach, kept running towards the door and got away. Racing through the streets with handcuffs dangling from one hand, Edwards signaled for help from a police car that was being driven by Rolf Mueller and Robert Rauth from the Milwaukee police division.

Edwards drove the policemen to Dahmer's home, where Dahmer initially was polite to the officers. Then Edwards recalled the knife that he knew Dahmer had in the room. One police officer checked the bedroom and he saw the photos of mutilated bodies. He shouted to his partner to capture Dahmer. While one officer overpowered Dahmer, the second opened the refrigerator to find a human skull. A further search of the house resulted in finding three more severed heads, various photos of dead men and human remains, dismembered penises and hands, as well as photos of eviscerated victims and human parts in his fridge.

The tale of Dahmer's apprehension and the items found in his apartment rapidly gained the public's attention. Some bodies were found in acid-filled barrels, and human heads were discovered in his closet. Investigation soon confirmed the extent of Dahmer's necrophilia and savagery. Seven severed heads were discovered in the apartment and a human heart was chilling in the freezer.

The doors of flat 213, both interior and exterior, were tightly secured with numerous locks and an alerting device. In the room and in the lobby were found photos and publications of male nudes captured in certain poses and obviously meant to be appealing to homosexual men.

There were also empty beer cans and dirty

dishes, as well as various obscene films lying around, for the most part of the particular kind made in California. The titles that Dahmer had included were: Chippendale's Tall Dark and Handsome, Cocktales, Rock Hard, Tropical Heat Wave, Hard Men II, Hard Men III, and Peep Show. Other non-sexual recordings included two that would be alluded to during the trial: Return of the Jedi and Exorcist II. A scene from Bill Cosby Show was also found on a tape.

On the kitchen floor there were four boxes of muriatic acid. The fridge contained, besides a man's head, some blood drops on the base, and in the freezer compartment there were three plastic sacks. Two sacks each had a heart, and the third had muscles. On another wall, there was a fridge in which three more skulls were discovered and a plastic sack containing a human torso. On the base of this freezer, there was another plastic pack with a substance which seemed to have flesh and different human organs.

The medical examiner determined that this whole freezer ought to be sealed and removed, with contents intact, in order to be examined later. In the hallway was a closet containing various chemicals and two bleached skulls. On the floor at the rear, there was an aluminum stockpot with two human hands that appeared to be from the same individual, since they looked similar, and human private parts including the penis and testicles.

The room had a single-size bed with a mattress red with blood, and more blood on the walls. Under the bed was the large knife about which Edwards had warned the cops. There was a Polaroid camera on top of the bed, and beside the bed there was a metal file cabinet. When it was opened, the top drawer held three human skulls on a dark towel.

The cops saw these skulls had been colored green with dark specks. However, the medical examiner explained that they were colored and coated to 'a dim marble-like surface', and the towel was dull blue. The bottom drawer contained an entire human skeleton, and in front of it there were two paper sacks; one had some dried portions of a human scalp, and the other had private parts, dried and mummified.

On the floor next to a chest, there was a case with a Styrofoam top which held two more heads, and in the corner there was a 57-gallon plastic drum that had a tightly fitting lid which was later found to contain three human torsos in different stages of disintegration. Inside the chest which Rolf Mueller had discovered open when he entered the room were original photos of an especially repellent nature. Upon checking, it was noted that there were 74 of them.

The bits and pieces of Dahmer's life were marked, recorded and removed with great care. A photograph collection, a ceramic coffee mug, an empty Budweiser can, an empty Paramount rum bottle, an empty paper lunch-bag lying on a table near the sofa in the living room - the delicate flotsam and jetsam of normal life rubbing against the iniquitous and the evil.

A couple of things were important, but they weren't uncovered until later. One large hypodermic needle seemed puzzling, and a contact lens cleaning kit that was quite harmless. Two plastic gargoyle figures were recovered from the living room and chemical-safe gloves lay beside gallons of muriatic acid and six boxes of Soilex cleaner.

Beside a drill and drill bits, a saw and a claw hammer, there were other items which suggested goodness and decency.

For instance, there was a King James Bible, tapes about Creation Science, tapes on such topics as The Genesis Flood, Age of the Earth and Science. Furthermore, there were also tapes on Numerology and the Divine Triangle, as well as a learning unit with tapes on Latin. There were four books concerning the care of aquariums and fish as well as a pristine aquarium with graceful exotic fish and live plants.

***

The main individual who given the task of plumbing the depths of Dahmer's depravity was Detective Patrick Kennedy. A large man with a splendid handlebar moustache, he was the one to whom Dahmer discussed the finer points of his 13 years of murder.

Dahmer had fantasies about slaying men and about having intercourse with their bodies from the time he was 14 years old. However, he didn't on them until he graduated high school in June 1978. That's when he met the hitchhiker Steven Hicks. At the time, Dahmer was living with his parents in Bath, Ohio. They engaged in sexual activities and drank some beer. When Hicks was ready to be on his way, Dahmer couldn't bear the thought of Hicks leaving, so he hit him on the head with a dumbbell and killed him.

He had to dispose of the body, so he cut it into pieces, bundled it up in plastic trash bags and hid the bags in the woods behind his home. That fall he went to Ohio State University for one semester but failed. In late 1978, Dahmer joined the Army and shipped out to Germany. A thorough investigation reveals that he didn't murder anybody in the Army. He was discharged from the Army after two years because of his alcoholism. When he got home, he retrieved Hicks's body, beat the remains with a heavy maul and scattered the results throughout the woods.

The security measures for Dahmer's trial was extraordinary in the history of Milwaukee. The court was swept daily for bombs, using specially trained dogs to sniff for explosives. Each person who entered the courtroom was searched and checked using a metal detector. Inside the court, an eight-foot-high-bullet-proof barrier was installed to separate Dahmer from the public.

There were 100 accessible seats; 23 were for journalists; 34 for the families of Dahmer's victims; and the remainder for the public. The leading participants in this legal production, other than Dahmer himself, were District Attorney Michael McCann, Judge Laurence Gram, Jr., guards, and the defense attorney Gerald Boyle, who had defended Dahmer in his prior trial. Lionel and Shari went to court each day.

On July 13, 1992, Dahmer disregarded his lawyer's advice and changed his plea to guilty, based on his claim of insanity. As noted by Don

Davis in 'The Milwaukee Murders', this action upset his entire defense. Rather than proving his client didn't commit the murders, Lawyer Boyle unrolled one of the most bizarre tapestries ever to grace an American court. His job was to persuade the jury that the suspect was insane, since only a crazy person would do what he did. McCann wanted to demonstrate that he was not lawfully crazy – and that although he recognized his deeds were not right, he did it at any rate. Dahmer was an underhanded mental case who attracted his casualties and killed them without hesitating.

The potential jury pool was warned, "You're going to find out about things you most likely never knew existed in this present reality." For this situation Boyle let them know, "you're going to find out about sexual conduct before death, during death, and after death." Boyle and McCann eliminated potential jurors who discriminated against gay people or who did not trust expert witnesses or psychiatrists.

On January 29, 1992, the jury and two alternates were chosen. A single black juror was chosen, which caused a furor among the victims' families. The whole case was grounded along racial lines. Soon, it appeared as if this jury of six white men and seven white women was simply one more case of racial foul play.

It is not unusual for necrophiliacs is practice cannibalism. Dahmer asserted that he consumed the flesh of his victims because he thought they would still live through him. Dahmer experimented with different seasonings to improve the taste of human flesh. Eating it brought on an erection. His notorious freezer contained pieces of frozen human flesh. He tasted human blood as well, but he didn't like it.

He wanted to maintain some of his kills with preservation and taxidermy. Control was essential for Dahmer. He couldn't endure desertion or rejection. Indeed, even in his personal connections as a homosexual, he would not try to satisfy his sexual partner; he was only interested in his personal satisfaction which consisted of oral or anal sex on his partner, alive or dead.

This requirement for control led him to some radical theories. One was a crude form of lobotomy which he tried on a few of his victims. While the victim was drugged, he made a hole in his skull and inserted some muriatic acid into his brain. Of course, the recipient died quickly, although one of them had some minimal function for a brief time before dying.

It is only to be expected that his need for control would include dabbling with Satanism.

Indeed, simply having pieces of his victims close by gave him a sense of wickedness. "I have to question whether or not there is an evil force in the world and whether or not I have been influenced by it," said Dahmer. "Although I am not sure if there is a God or if there is a devil, I know that as of lately, I have been doing a lot of thinking about both." He intended to erect a shrine in his apartment to highlight many of his trophies, the statue of a griffin, as well as burning incense in the skulls of his victims, with the goal of acquiring special powers and energies to assist him both socially and fiscally.

Dahmer was accused of 17 counts of murder, later lowered to 15. He was never charged for the attempted murder of Edwards. Dahmer's trial started on January 30, 1992. Even with proof against him, he still insisted he was not liable because he was insane. The trial went on for two weeks.

The Court declared Dahmer to be sane and guilty of 15 of the murder charges. The judge sentenced him to 15 life terms, for a total of 957 years in jail, which is the most severe punishment permitted by Wisconsin law. The death penalty has not been available in that state since 1853. During the sentencing hearing, Dahmer expressed regret for his actions and said he longed for his own death. In May of that year, he was removed to Ohio where he entered a guilty plea for the death of his first victim, Stephen Hicks.

Dahmer was incarcerated in the Columbia Correctional Institution in Portage, Wisconsin. This is where he announced that he was a born-again Christian. Roy Ratcliff, a local minister from the Churches of Christ, was able to meet Dahmer and baptize him.

Dahmer was assaulted twice while in prison, first in July 1994. A prisoner tried to slice Dahmer's throat with a sharp weapon as Dahmer was coming back to his cell from a service in the chapel. He managed to get away from the confrontation with minor injuries. Then on November 28, 1994, he and another prisoner, Jesse Anderson, were performing janitorial tasks in the prison gymnasium when they were seriously beaten with a broomstick by prisoner Christopher Scarver. Dahmer died of severe head injuries en route to the hospital. Two days later, Anderson also died as a result of his injuries.

Jesse Anderson's injuries were a direct result of having his skull repeatedly bashed against the walls and floor. His injuries were compared to those received in an auto crash. Scarver's motive? "God made me do it," he said. He got another lifelong incarceration for his trouble. Jeffrey was cremated, and Dahmer's parents, after fighting each other in court, each got half of his ashes.

Chapter 5: Gary Ridgway

"I don't believe in man, God, or the Devil. I hate the whole damned human race, including myself."
- Gary Ridgway

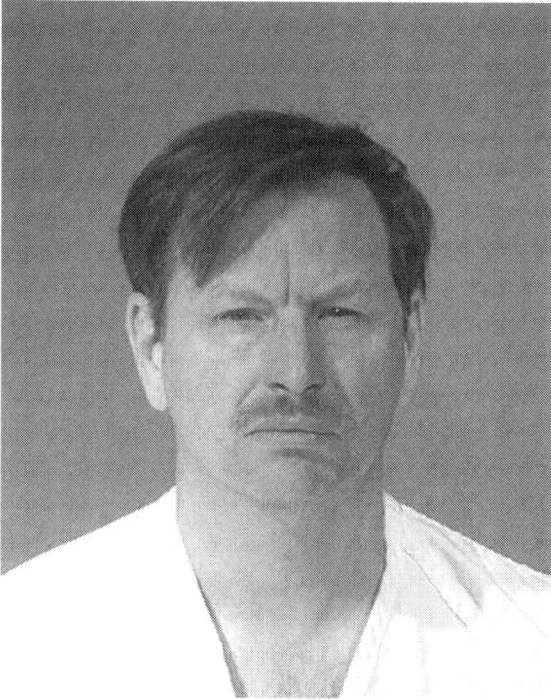

Also known as Green River Killer, Gary Leon Ridgway is one of the most recognized serial killers in the world. From the 1980s to 1990s, Gary claimed the lives of a great many women in

Washington. His nickname, Green River Killer, was because his first five victims were discovered in the Green River. Gary Ridgway killed his victims by strangling them, often using his bare hands but sometimes by using ligatures. He then dumped their bodies all over the overgrown and wooded areas in King County.

Gary was working at a Kenworth Truck Factory in Renton, Washington. On November 30, 2001, he was apprehended for the murders of four women whose deaths were linked to him via DNA evidence. Gary agreed to provide information about the other missing women as part of a plea agreement which would spare him from the death penalty and instead he would be given a sentence of life imprisonment without parole. Gary's particular characteristics were both necrophilia and rape. In total, authorities accounted for 49 murders, though, according to Gary's account, the number was greater than 49. On December 18, 2003, he was sentenced to 48 years in prison.

***

Gary Leon Ridgway was born on February 18, 1949, in Salt Lake City, Utah. His parents were Thomas Newton Ridgway and Mary Rita Steinman. Gary had two brothers, Thomas Edward and Gregory Leon. They were raised in the McMicken Height area near SeaTac, in Washington.

Gary Ridgway's early life was not smooth at all and was more than a bit disturbing. Gary's relatives described his mother as domineering. They also claimed that Gary witnessed violent arguments between his parents. As a young boy, Ridgway would sometimes wet his bed. His mother would humiliate him before the family members. His mother would bathe him and clean up the mess though she never failed to belittle Gary and embarrass him before every family member. All these conflicting feelings caused Gary to fluctuate between anger and sexual attraction towards his mother.

During his young age, Ridgway was tested with the result indicating an IQ of 82, signifying low intelligence. Gary's performances at school was poor at best. At some point, Gary repeated a class two times in order to get the grades needed to pass on to the next class. He studied at Tyee Secondary School where his classmates described him as highly forgettable but congenial.

Gary's teenage years were troubled, and a notable instance of his killing nature was when he was 16. Gary stabbed a six-year-old boy several times in the ribs and in the liver. The boy survived the attack. Gary had led the boy to the

93

woods where he stabbed him. According to the victim and confirmed by Gary, after the act, Ridgway walked away laughing and saying that he had always wondered what it would feel like to kill someone.

At the age of 18, Gary, while still in high school, joined the Navy. After his graduation, he married his 19-year-old high school sweetheart, Claudia Barrows. He was sent to Vietnam where he worked on board a supply ship.

During his stay in the military, he started investing a considerable measure of energy with whores and contracted gonorrhea for the second time. This maddened him, yet he kept on having unprotected sex with them. During this time, his young wife, Claudia, only 19, started dating once more, and the marriage collapsed within a year.

Since she had loved him once, she spoke about him after his arrest and portrayed him as friendly but weird. His initial two marital unions ended in divorce because both partners were unfaithful. His second wife, Marcia Winslow, asserted that he had put her in a chokehold. He became fanatically religious during his second marriage, going door to door to share his beliefs, studying the Bible loudly at home and at work, and demanding that Marcia obey the strictures of their church minister.

Ridgway would often cry following sermons or Bible reading. However, Ridgway continued to seek the services of prostitutes throughout this marriage. Furthermore, Gary needed Marcia to take part in sex in public and in unsuitable locations, sometimes even in areas where his murdered victims' corpses had been found.

As indicated by the Time Magazine essayist Terry McCarthy, Gary had a voracious need for sex. His three exes and a few former girlfriends said that Ridgway required sex from them several times each day. He would insist on engaging in sexual relations in public areas or in the wooded areas. Ridgway himself confessed to having an obsession with prostitutes, who he both loved and hated. He often opposed their presence in his community, while at the same time seeking out their services. It's conceivable that Ridgway was conflicted between his voracious desires and his strong religious convictions. In 1975, his second wife delivered his child, Matthew.

***

All through the 1980s and also 1990s, he is said to have killed no less than 71 women as admitted by Ridgway himself in a meeting with Sheriff Reichert in 2001, in the Seattle-Tacoma area in Washington. Gary's statements in court later indicated that he had murdered so many women that he lost count. A greater part of the killings happened between 1982 and 1984.

Victims were said to be either prostitutes or runaway girls he picked up around the Pacific Highway South. A great many of their bodies were dumped in lush regions encompassing the Green River, except for two confirmed and another two presumed victims who were located in Portland, Oregon. The bodies were usually left in groups, often posed, and typically naked.

In some instances, he would come back to the victims' corpses and engage in sexual relations with them. Since many of the corpses were not found until they were reduced to skeletons, four of the victims are yet unidentified. Gary Ridgway sometimes scattered gum or cigarette butts over the area and mixed the materials with existing trash. He took some of the victims' corpses over the state border into Oregon to mislead the police.

Ridgway started every murder by picking up a female, usually a prostitute. Sometimes he showed the woman a photo of his child to gain her trust. After engaging in sexual relations with them, Ridgway choked them from behind. At first he choked them using his arm. However, sometimes the victims left wounds on his arms as they tried to defend themselves. These injuries and wounds would draw attention so Ridgway started using ligatures to choke his victims. The majority of his victims were murdered in his residence, his vehicle, or a remote area.

In the mid-1980s, King County Sheriff's Department assembled a Green River Task Force to focus on the killings. The most prominent individuals on the team were Robert Keppel and Dave Reichert. Dave occasionally met with serial killer, Ted Bundy, starting from 1984. The meetings with Bundy were not much help in the Green River investigation. John E. Douglas, who afterward contributed much information about the Green River Killer, also was involved.

Ridgway was apprehended in 1982 and again in 2001 on charges connected to prostitution. He was a suspect in 1983 in the Green River deaths. In 1984, Gary Ridgway took and passed a polygraph examination, and on April 7, 1987, law enforcement officers collected hair and saliva samples from Gary Ridgway. Around 1985, Gary Ridgway started dating Judith Mawson and she became his third wife in 1988. In 2010, Mawson stated that when she moved to his home while they were still dating, there were no carpets. Analysts later informed her that Gary had likely wrapped a body using the carpets. In that same meeting, she told how he would leave in the early morning and be gone for many hours or for many days, apparently for additional time pay.

Mawson surmised that he probably dedicated a portion of this time to the homicides while she thought he was working these early morning shifts. She insisted that she had no suspicions of Ridgway's criminal acts prior to his encounters with law enforcement in 1987. She didn't know, in any case, about the Green River Killer earlier since she didn't listen to the news.

Pennie Morehead said that when she talked with Ridgway in jail, he said his murderous urges were diminished while he was with his wife Mawson, so that he committed fewer murders than he might otherwise have done and that he really loved her. Mawson told a local journalist that she felt she had saved many lives by being Gary's wife and keeping him happy.

The samples gathered in 1987 were next submitted for DNA testing, forming the basis for his arrest warrant. On November 30, 2001, Gary was at Kenworth Truck production line, where he worked as a painter, when police arrived there to take him into custody. Ridgway was arrested on suspicion of the murder of four women about 20 years earlier who had only now been identified. He was considered as a potential suspect when the DNA positively matched the semen left behind in victims to the saliva swab taken by the policemen.

The four victims mentioned in the first indictment were Opal Mills, Marcia Chapman, Carol Ann Christensen and Cynthia Hinds. Three more victims, Debra Bonner, Debra Estes, and Wendy Coffield, were added to the indictment after a forensic scientist determined that some minute paint spray particles were from a product used at the Kenworth plant during the time frame when these women were killed.

In April 2001, some 20 years after the original Green River deaths, Detective Reichert, was now the sheriff of King County. He directed the Task Force to re-examine the homicide investigation. It was a case he declined to relinquish as he was determined to discover the killer. This time the team had innovation on their side.

Reichert formed another team group, at first comprising six individuals, including DNA specialists and a few criminologists. As the team developed, it comprised more than 30 individuals. All the materials from the murder investigation were looked at again and some of the specimens was sent to the labs.

The main samples to be sent to the lab were found on three victims that were killed somewhere around 1982 and 1983: Opal Mills, Marcia Chapman and Carol Christensen. The specimens comprised semen taken from the victims. The semen samples were subjected to a new DNA testing technique and were compared with samples taken from Ridgway in April 1987.

***

In the first months of 1987, agents had another suspect in connection to the Green River murders. Already known to the police, he came to their attention when he solicited an undercover officer posing as a prostitute in May 1984. Anyway, the man was discharged after he effectively breezed through a polygraph test. When examiners looked further into the man's past, they found that he had been reported for choking a prostitute in 1980 near the Sea-Tac International Airport. However, the man argued self-defense after swearing the lady bit him. He was released from police custody.

One of the team investigators, Matt Haney, was exceptionally suspicious of Ridgway as a suspect and chose to inquire significantly into the man's history. He found that the police had once pulled the man over and interviewed him in 1982 while Gary was in his truck with a prostitute. Haney discovered that the prostitute he was with was one of the ladies on the Green River kill list, Keli McGinness.

Haney found out from the man's ex that he regularly frequented the dumpsites where a significant number of the bodies had been found. Likewise, a few prostitutes swore to have seen a man resembling his description who routinely visited the strip somewhere around 1982 and 1983. As it happened, the man passed that strip day after day on his commute to work. The most significant confirmation was that the man, who worked as a truck painter, was found to have been taking a sick day or a vacation day each time a victim vanished.

At last, on April 8th, 1987, the police got a warrant and looked into the man's home. As indicated by the Seattle Times, the police likewise took "fresh" DNA samples so they could compare them against the evidence they had from the Green River victims. In any case, there was not enough evidence to take him in and the man was discharged from the police custody. The suspect was identified as Gary Ridgway.

A few weeks after Ridgway's discharge, Captain Pompey succumbed to a massive heart attack connected with a scuba-diving incident. The tragic occasion was grabbed up by the media and sensationalized. It was proposed that the Green River Killer was actually a cop who had killed Pompey, paying little heed to the fact that there was not a shred of proof to bolster the hypothesis. One daily paper even demanded an official investigation concerning Pompey's death. It appeared as though the citizens' nerves were badly frayed after so much death in the city.

The team, now headed up by Captain Greg Boyle, was called on a day in June. Three young men searching for aluminum cans had unearthed a woman's remains. The young woman, identified as Cindy Ann Smith, 17, was found in a gorge in back of the Green River Community College. She had been missing for about three years at the time of her recovery.

More missing women were discovered in 1988, including that of runaway Debbie Gonzales, 14, and Debra Estes, aged 15, who had vanished six years earlier. Their deaths were ascribed to the Green River Killer. In spite of the fact that there were still bodies being found, there were no recent murders being attributed to the Green River Killer in Seattle.

In 1988, the finding of the bodies of more than 20 prostitutes in San Diego indicated perhaps that the Green River Killer had moved on and continued with his crime spree in California. Reichert and the new task force leader Bob Evans contacted the San Diego police department to join their efforts to catch the killer. In December 1988, investigators had another suspect.

A man named William J. Stevens came to the attention of the police after several citizens called to suggest his name following an episode of Crime Stoppers. Stevens had been running for eight years, after he escaped during a two-year term in a correctional facility for burglary. He was enrolled at the University of Washington as a pharmacology student at the time of his rediscovery.

As a team of specialists dug into Stevens's past, they discovered that he was already a suspect in the Green River killings. It was likewise discovered that Stevens had an open disdain for prostitutes and was known to have, on a few occasions, mentioned killing them. When police looked into his home, they discovered multiple guns, a few drivers' licenses, charge cards and sexually explicit photographs of prostitutes. Stevens had mostly been into burglary and charge card fraud, which were his means of survival.

Task force agents thoroughly questioned

Stevens about the Green River murders and kept an eye on the premises of his home all through the late spring and fall of 1989. Agents even searched Stevens's father's home for any bit of information which could connect him to any of the killings. However, nothing was discovered to connect him to the homicides.

Also, Visa records and photos provided by Stevens's brother gave an unbreakable alibi. As per the various records and receipts, Stevens was travelling during the summer of 1982 when many of the murders took place. In the long run, Stevens was cleared of all suspicion in the Green River murders.

In October 1989, skeletal remains of two more women were found. One of the victims, identified as Andrea Childers, was found in an empty park near Star Lake and 55th Avenue South. In the same way as other young women were found before her, the cause of death was obscured because of the advanced state of decomposition. Toward the beginning of February 1990, Denise Bush's skull was discovered in a wooded part of Southgate Park in Tukwila, Washington. The rest of Bush's body had been found in Oregon five years before.

By the end of the day, it appeared as though the murderer was intentionally moving the bones around for the purpose of baffling investigators. Task force agents were wearily starting to think that the killer had won. Police morale was very low.

As reported by the Seattle Times, by July 1991 the team was down to only one investigator, Tom Jensen. After nine years, some 49 victims and 15 million dollars, the team still had not caught the Green River Killer. The examination came to be known as the nation's biggest unsolved murder case. The case stayed inactive for another ten years.

On September 10, 2001, Reichert got news from the labs. There was a match between the semen taken from the victims and Ridgway. On November 30, Ridgway was apprehended by investigators on his route home from work and charged with four counts of aggravated murder.

The charges included Opal Mills, Marcia Chapman, Carol Christensen, and Cynthia Hinds, in which circumstantial evidence had been discovered linking him with her death. The killer that the investigators had hunted for two decades was at last in police custody. This time, he wouldn't get away.

Ridgway, initially born in Salt Lake, Utah, on February 18, 1949, worked for a computer company at the time of his capture. During the years of the homicides, he was a truck painter at the Kenworth production line in Renton, Washington. Ridgway possessed numerous trucks during that time, one of which was especially significant to investigators. As per Seattle's KING5 TV channel, a 1977 black Ford F-150 possessed by the suspect was reportedly associated with some of the victims. Today, the truck is still under scrutiny.

As indicated by Time Magazine's Terry McCarthy, Gary Ridgway had an abnormal sexual craving. His three exes and a few former girlfriends told the columnist that he was sexually voracious, requesting sex multiple times each day. Regularly, he would need to engage in sexual relations in an open region or in the forested areas, even in the ranges where several of the bodies had been found.

Ridgway was likewise known to have been fixated on prostitutes, an obsession that verged on a love and hate relationship. Neighbors knew him to continually grumble about prostitutes conducting business in his neighborhood, yet in the meantime, he availed himself of their services. It was conceivable that he was torn by his out-of-control lust and his religious convictions. McCarthy observes that one of his spouses has said that he turned into a religious fanatic, many times crying after listening to sermons and reading the Bible scriptures.

**

Ahead of schedule in August 2003, the Seattle TV news reported that Gary had been transferred from a maximum security prison at King County to an Airway Heights Minimum-Medium Security Level Jail. Various news sources reported that his legal counselors, led by Anthony Savage, were drawing up a plea agreement that would save him from the death penalty in exchange for his cooperation concerning some of the Green River murders.

On November 5th, 2003, Gary Ridgway entered a guilty plea to 48 charges of first-degree murder in accordance with the plea agreement he accepted in June. Ridgway clarified that the majority of his victims had been murdered in King County and that he moved the remains of two victims to a location near Portland, Oregon, to baffle the police.

Deputy prosecutor Jeffrey Baird stated in court that that agreement included the names of 41 victims who would not have been added to this case were it not for the plea agreement. The King County Prosecuting Attorney disclosed his reason for offering the plea bargain.

On December 18, 2003, Judge Richard Jones at the King County Superior Court sentenced Gary Ridgway to 48 consecutive life sentences with no possibility of parole. He received an extra 10 years for tampering with evidence for each of the 48 victims, adding 480 more years to his 48 life sentences.

Gary Ridgway directed prosecutors to three bodies in 2003. On August 16th that year, the remains of 16-year-old Pammy Annette Avent were found close to Enumclaw, 40 feet from State Route 410. Authorities previously believed she had been a victim of the Green River Killer. The remains of Marie Malvar and April Buttram were were revealed in September. On November 23, 2005, Associated Press said that a weekend hiker found a skull belonging to one of the 48 women that Ridgway admitted killing in his 2003 plea deal with the King County prosecutors. This was found to be the head of Tracy Winston, who was 19 years old when she vanished from Northgate Mall on September 12, 1983, and was found by a hiker in a wooded area close to Highway 18 near Issaquah, southeast of Seattle.

Ridgway has confessed to more confirmed killings than any other American serial murderer. Over a timespan of five months, he admitted to

48 killings. Forty-two of these were on the policemen's running list of suspected Green River Killer victims. On February 9, 2004, the area prosecutors started to release the tape recordings of Ridgway's admissions.

In one taped session, he told agents that he was responsible for the deaths of 65 women. However, in another taped meeting with Reichert on December 31, 2003, Gary Ridgway claimed he killed 71 victims and admitted to having had sex with them before killing them. These things were not revealed until after the sentencing. He admitted that he focused on prostitutes since they were easy to pick up and that he hated so many of them. He also said he had sexual intercourse with his victims' bodies after he killed them, yet he affirmed he started burying the later victims so he would not be tempted to commit necrophilia.

Ridgway conversed with and attempted to put his victims at ease before he killed them. He said he would talk to them, get their mind off of sex or anything they were uncomfortable about. They thought that he cared, which he didn't. All that he wanted was to get them into his truck so he could kill them. Ridgway stated that killing young women was his "career". Gary Ridgway was housed in solitary confinement at Washington State Penitentiary in Walla Walla in

January 2004. He is permitted out of his cell for one hour four times a week. About 2005, Ridgway filed more requests with the federal government and was exchanged to Airway Heights where he was placed in a base medium security jail.

On May 14, 2015, he was exchanged to the USP Florence, a high-security federal prison, east of Canon City, Colorado. In September 2015, after an open objection and conversations with Governor Jay Inslee, Corrections Secretary Bernie Warner declared that Gary Ridgway would be exchanged back to Washington State Penitentiary to be easily accessible for open murder investigations. Ridgway was returned by a sanctioned plane to Washington from the High-Security Federal Prison in Florence, Colorado, on October 24, 2015.

Chapter 6: Edmund Kemper

When asked what he thought when he saw a pretty
girl walking down the street, Kemper replied:
"One side of me says, 'I'd like to talk to her, date her.'
The other side of me says, 'I wonder how her head
would look on a stick."
- Ed Kemper

Also known as Co-ed Killer, Edmund Kemper
was a serial killer. Edmund was actively killing in
the 1970s. His killing and his criminal life started

when he was still a teenager. He shot both his grandparents while he was staying with them at their ranch, located in North Fork, California. Edmund was incarcerated for these crimes. Later on, Edmund murdered six female hitchhikers and dismembered them in the Santa Cruz area, California. In addition, Edmund killed his mother and her friend and, after this, he gave himself up to the authorities.

***

He was born in the Burbank area in California on December 18, 1948. He was the son of Edmund Emil and Clarnell Stage. Edmund turned out to be very intelligent, his IQ being 136. Edmund, however, showed signs of sociopathic characteristics from the time he was very young. He used to torture and kill animals; he acted out some strange sexual rituals using his sister's dolls. Edmund once said that if he wanted to kiss a tutor whom he adored, he would have to kill him first. His mother exacerbated the situation by humiliating him. She made him live down in a basement because she feared that Edmund might molest his sisters. She had a borderline personality disorder that made her angry and abusive to her son.

Edmund was never content to live on the farm with his grandparents. During school, he seemed very quiet and never caused any trouble. He scored average grades. At home, Edmund spent most of the time with his dog as well as with a .22 gun that was given to him. He used to shoot rabbits, as well as birds. Though warned against it, he continued to do so and it was clear that he was becoming more aggressive. After school, Edmund went to his mother to spend some time there during summer, but after two weeks he returned to the farm. He found his grandparents and the farm boring, and while on the farm, Edmund thought of what it might be like to kill.

Edmund Kemper killed his 66-year-old grandmother in August 1964 when she was in her kitchen. He shot her while she was finalizing the children's writings she was working with. After Edmund's grandfather returned home from shopping, he shot him too. Edmund called his mother and asked her what he should do. She told him to call the police. When Edmund was asked why, he said he just wanted to know what it felt like to kill his grandmother. He said that the reason for killing his grandfather was that he would be mad at him for killing his grandmother. Consequently, Edmund Kemper was taken to a hospital at Atascadero State. There, he befriended a psychologist and he even became an assistant to that psychologist.

Edmund was very intelligent and thus he managed to gain the trust of doctors. This trust gave him access to the prisoners' records and tests. He impressed the doctors so much that he was later released to the care of his mother in Santa Cruz, although this was all against some other doctors' advice. He had convinced the psychologists he was fit, then he went even further to get his juvenile documents sealed forever.

At the hospital, Edmund had a chance to understand serial killers and rapists, among others. They shared stories of crime with him. This made him rapidly aware of sexuality and this was quickly linked to domination and violence. As a result, his sexual fantasies and violence increased. Again, he learned about the things which enabled the rapists around there to be caught, and he realized that they were arrested for not being smart enough to hide the evidence or get rid of witnesses. He also learned that they assaulted women they knew very well or, even worse, they did the act in public. He saved all these discoveries in his mind because he knew that one day this would help him, though he had no plan at the moment. He never shared any of these fantasies with the doctors and only displayed hard work and good behaviors.

He believed in religious conversion and thus he always looked up any biblical quote he came across or heard. Edmund was clean-cut, sheltered and intelligent. Upon release, he saw huge changes on the outside. He quickly renewed his contact with the outer world and enrolled in the Atascadero Community College. Here he attended classes, though Edmond was still under the watchful eye of the youth authority. He wished to become a law enforcer; he maintained short hair and a neatly trimmed moustache. This was not to happen because his height never met the requirements of the local or state agencies. Thus he thought to buy a motorcycle so that he could feel like a cop. His return to his mother in Santa Cruz was very much against the advice of doctors at Atascadero, but the youth authorities gave him back to his mother.

***

His mother had an administrative position in the University of California. The absence of her son, Edmund, gave her some measure of peace. Edmund had loud battles and fights with his mother so that neighbors could hear them often. Edmund would often seek refuge in the Jury Room which was a local bar that was frequented by law enforcement officers. He liked them a lot and spent hours talking about various types of ammunition and guns, their merits and shortcomings. He was respectful to these law enforcement officers and they used to call him Big Ed.

Edmund used to pick up odd jobs and labors until he managed to get a job at the Division of Highways. This enabled him to move from his mother's house to an apartment located in Alameda. He shared this apartment with a friend. Edmund claimed later that his mother continued to belittle him and this caused him to wreck his motorcycle two times. The Division of Highways, therefore, gave him some time off so that he could recover from his broken arm. Using his out-of-court fund, Edmund managed to buy a car exactly the same as that of a policeman. He incorporated radio receivers and a microphone, as well as a big antenna. This is when he began picking up hitchhikers. He used to notice how the hitchhikers reacted to him, and he gained their trust by safely delivering them to their destinations. Edmund began indulging in his prior fantasies and envisioned what he intended to do to them once he had taken care of everything. He decided to change his car to fit his future plans. He removed the antenna and modified the doors so that they could not be opened from the inside.

Edmund placed knives, guns, plastic bags and blankets in his car trunk. He picked up a girl only as an experiment to his plan, waiting for the appropriate time to arrive. This took some time, about a year, before he could actually utilize the plan he had.

Finally on May 7, 1972, the time arrived and Edmund began using his plan. Anita Luchese and Mary Pesce were students from Fresno College. They were both hitchhiking to the University of Stanford and then a few days later to Berkeley. The girls never reached where they were going. They were both reported missing. It was hard for the police to locate them because they were runaways and transients. It was common for girls to go missing, but later they would usually turn up.

Edmund drove the girls around, and after some time he took out the gun and stopped the car in a remote area. He placed Anita in the car trunk and focused his full attention to Mary Ann. Edmund handcuffed her and laid her in the back seat of his car. He tried to strangle her using a towel with a plastic bag around her head. Mary Ann made an opening in the bag and Edmund was frustrated by this act. He now took a knife and stabbed Mary Ann many times and later on slashed her throat. Afterward, he got Anita from the car trunk and began stabbing her. Anita screamed and fought, but eventually Edmund managed to subdue her.

Edmund drove with the bodies of the two in the car while he was contemplating what to do next. He brought Mary Ann's body to his apartment and started dissecting her. Later Edmund beheaded the body of Anita. He buried the body of Mary Ann using the plastic bag he had attempted to suffocate her with. Edmund later led the police to the scene, but he preserved the heads for some time before throwing them in a ravine. Mary Ann's head was found and recognized in August, but nothing concerning Anita was ever seen.

Nobody ever suspected Edmund of anything suspicious and thus allowed him to continue with his acts. On September 14, 1972, he took a 15-year-old dancer named Aiko Koo of Korean descent. She was going to dance classes and was tired of waiting for a bus and thus decided to hitchhike. The girl realized Edmund's plan and panicked, but he convinced her that the purpose of the gun was to kill himself. He warned her of signaling anyone and assured her that she would not be harmed if she remained silent. Edmund drove into the hills and then left the main road. He parked the car out of sight, then he taped the mouth of the girl and attempted to suffocate her placing his thumb on her nostril. The girl fought Edmund, but soon she lost consciousness. A moment later the girl woke up and Edmund continued suffocating her until she stopped breathing. Edmund then took her from his car and laid her flat down and raped her.

Using her own scarf, Edmund suffocated her and, after confirming that she was dead, he placed her in the trunk and drove off. He stopped at a nearby bar and got some beer before heading to his mother's home. He occasionally opened the trunk and gazed at his victim. Later on, he brought Aiko's corpse into his house and dissected her the same way he did with Anita and Mary Ann. He disposed of her body in various locations, other than the hands and her head. Little was discovered about her, and this incident was never linked to that of Mary Ann and Anita.

After four months, there was a discovery of bodies disposed of by other killers. This raised public concerns, but Edmund was not even close to a suspect. In January 1973, Edmund bought a .22 automatic gun. He was not allowed to own a firearm due to his prior crimes, but he proceeded to purchase it. Purchasing the firearm was an easy process, but he still worried that later the authorities might discover him and charge him for the illegal possession of a gun.

From that day on, he increased his kills. Cindy Schall was another victim; he drove to the hills and forced her into his trunk and then shot her with his new gun. Because he had moved into his mother's house, Edmund brought Cindy's body to the duplex in Aptos, then into his room. When his mother left for work the following day, he had sexual relations with the corpse. He later dissected Cindy's body in the bathtub. Edmund then took great care to wipe all the surfaces he had touched. He removed the bullet from Cindy's head and buried her head in his mother's backyard. Later he placed the body in a plastic bag and threw it off the cliff. Cindy's body was found within 24 hours, and Edmund noticed this, but with nothing to worry about, he was prepared to kill again. Edmund was sure of the careful steps he was taking.

Clarnell and Edmund had an argument and he stormed out of his mother's house. He stopped to pick up Rosalind, at first engaging her in a conversation. Later he stopped and picked up another hitchhiker named Alice. She never had a problem getting into the car since Rosalind was in it already and it displayed a UC Santa Cruz parking sticker. Edmund didn't even stop the car to kill. He only directed Rosalind's attention to the passenger side. As Rosalind was looking, Edmund slowly reached for his gun and shot her in the head. He again fast pointed the gun to Alice and shot her several times. Unlike Rosalind, Alice didn't die at once. He stopped after a while and transferred the corpses to the trunk.

Then Edmund stopped for gas and later he headed to his mother's house, then left hurriedly claiming that he needed cigarettes. Upon arrival at his apartment, he opened the car trunk and then beheaded the corpses. The following day, in the morning, Edmund brought in Alice's corpse and had sexual relations with it. He then brought in Rosalind's head so that he could dispose of the bullet the same way he did with Cindy. He then again drove off to Santa Cruz to dispose of the bodies. Later he drove to Pacifica to dispose of the hands and heads.

Edmund's mother never seemed to have any suspicion about her son. She never suspected that she would become a victim. A month after killing Rosalind and Alice, Edmund decided to kill his mother. He waited in his room until his mother slept soundly. At around 5 a.m., he went to the kitchen and got a hammer. He went to his mother's bedroom and hit her head with the hammer, then slashed her throat. Within no time, he had killed her and beheaded her. He had removed the larynx and tried to push it in the garbage disposal, but it kept on coming back. This surprised Edmund not at all; he found it rather ironic. He placed her corpse in the closet, cleaned up the house and left.

In the afternoon, he wondered what to do. He thought that if someone else was dead in the same place with his mother, then it would direct suspicion away from him. He went back to his mother's house and called Sara (Sally) Hallett, his mother's friend, and invited her to dinner that evening. Upon her arrival, he strangled her manually at first and later used the scarf that he got from Aiko. He removed Sara's clothes and carried her body to the bed where he tried to engage in sexual acts with her.

On Sunday morning, he went to town driving Sara's car. Then he rented a car to avoid being noticed and dropped Sara's auto at a certain gas station. He told the assistant at the gas station that the car needed to be repaired. Edmund drove for about 18 hours, and he only stopped for gas and some soda. In Colorado, he was even stopped for speeding and he was very calm. He paid the fine charged and proceeded with the journey. After a long run, he became tired and stopped at

Pueblo. He called the Santa Cruz police department and started confessing all eight murders.

***

The Santa Cruz police would never believe that the man who was calling to confess the murders was the same man they used to be friends with, Big Ed. He explained that after leaving his mother's house, he drove for hours after dropping the car he had and then renting another one. This was when he decided to turn himself in. He talked about other murder cases that the police had not resolved yet. The officer who picked up his first call believed that someone was playing a prank with them. The officer told him to call again sometime later.

Edmund had a hard time convincing the officer that he was telling the truth and wanted them to take him seriously. Individuals who knew him thought he was joking around. He continued making calls until he managed to convince an officer to go and check on his mother. He referred to Sergeant Aluffi who had been there earlier on to confiscate the rifle he had. So the sergeant went to Edmund's home, and as he entered the house, he could smell some odor of decomposition. After opening the closet, the sergeant saw blood and some hair. He then called the detective after securing the place. Upon arrival, they were amazed to find two bodies exactly the way Edmund had told them.

They realized that during the time Edmund used to interact with them in the Jury Room, he was learning more about future strategies to be applied. He knew the plans that the officers would use to arrest him, so he eluded them. Edmund never came across as a killer, but rather as an attractive person. This enabled him to attract girls to his cars because they felt safe around him.

Edmund returned to Santa Cruz and there he led the investigators to the places in which he dumped the bodies of his victims. He again moved on to give all of his confessions. Edmund was very thorough in his confession so that James Jackson, the public defender, had no chance of defending Edmund except for an insanity defense. Various witnesses came to testify to Edmund's innocence, but the prosecutor dismissed all the witnesses. Dr. Joel Fort had spent quite some time in running through Edmund's case. He went even farther to the test results after he killed both of his grandparents. He again interviewed Edmund for his cannibalism and also the information on his sexual practices with the victims' bodies.

Edmund Kemper remains in custody. He was unlike another serial killer because he was eager to tell about the crimes he had committed. This gained much attention from a lot of people. He did intensive interviews with the FBI agent, Robert Ressler. This was aimed at helping the FBI build up a serial killer profile. During 1988, he and John Wayne Gacy both participated in the satellite broadcast where each one of them was required to discuss his crimes. He was very explicit and loquacious, and this showed how much psychological insight regarding his crimes he had gained. While in prison, Edmund was well behaved and very cooperative. He seemed to take pride in his being termed as a genius serial killer who assisted in his own capture. Edmund knew very well that his release would result in great tragedy. He has, therefore, assured himself that he is going nowhere.

***

Edmund was sentenced for eight counts of murder in May 1973. He was diagnosed as psychotic and one who had not been cured fully. This was against the psychiatric records that had pronounced him safe earlier on. Before trial, Edmund had attempted to commit suicide two times and failed on both. Dr. Joel Fort looked at Edmund's juvenile records and then examined the records which showed that he was diagnosed with psychosis. Dr. Joel Fort had a lengthy interview with Edmund, and he later told the court that Edmund was involved in an act of cannibalism.

He confessed that he had dissected parts of the girls and later cooked and ate them. The doctor additionally said that Edmund knew exactly what he was doing in every incident he was involved in. He also claimed that Edmund was thrilled by the notoriety of being a mass killer and knew very well that what he did was not good. He also displayed signs of clear planning and premeditation.

One of Edmund's defenders, a psychiatrist, intended to testify to his insanity based on the fact that the crime was a product of a diseased mind. However, this was against the state definition of 'Product Standard'. The prosecution experts also questioned the staff at Atascadero on Edmund's diagnosis at the time he was 15 years old. Edmund tried to explain how he felt about his state of mind. The fact that he needed a woman and his necrophilia act were indications that his mind was not in a good state. He also said that after the killing, he felt remorse and that resulted in too much drinking to relieve that feeling. Additionally, he said that the feeling he felt after beheading someone was like a narcotic.

***

The trial lasted for three weeks. Though all that Edmund had confessed was not clear whether it was true, Edmund later recanted what he had said earlier about cannibalism. He claimed that it was just for the insanity defense. On November 8, six men and six women in the jury discussed the case for about five hours. They finally concluded that Edmund was guilty of eight counts of first-degree murder. Kenmore hoped to get a death penalty. The Supreme Court had at that moment placed a moratorium on all capital punishment and all death sentences were transmuted to life imprisonment.

The death penalty only became applicable after January 1, 1974. According to Everitt, the jury questioned him on what his punishment should be. He came up with something that he had been thinking about for quite some time. Edmund told the judge that he ought to be punished by being tortured to death.

Edmund, contrary to his expectations, was sentenced to life imprisonment. He was taken to the California State Prison in Vacaville, in North San Francisco. After observation there, Edmund was taken to the maximum security prison

Cheney in Folsom. Edmund requested psychosurgery which involves inserting a probe in the brain to kill all the tissues that trigger compulsive aggression. Edmund's request was not accepted because the authorities feared that he might then claim his release. Edmund became a model inmate who assisted the blind by reading books on tape. The moment he went back to his parole hearing, he told them that he felt he was not fit to go back to the community.

In prison, Edmund was said to be kind as well as cooperative. He claimed that he wanted to forget about his past. Edmund readily and eagerly accepted examination and interviews. He hoped that he would assist others to learn about individuals like him. Later on, he disliked what some interviewers said about him.

FBI agent Robert Ressler became part of Behavioral Science as a specialist in Quantico. He went to prisons in order to interview notorious killers. He hoped to get useful information that could be helpful in solving crimes. This piece of information would allow them to have more knowledge about killers and would be used in a book that Douglas and his team were writing.

They contacted various prisoners. Ressler, who was an author, recounted a time when he was having an interview with Edmund. The session was lasting for quite some time. When Resseler pressed a button to call a guard, no one came. They continued some time, and after pressing the button the second time, still no one came. Ressler said that Kemper told him to relax and said that if he went mad there, Ressler would be in big trouble. Edmund said that he could twist off his head and place it on the table. Ressler asked him if he wouldn't get in trouble. Kemper replied, "What are they going to do, take away my TV privileges?"

Finally, when the guard came, Edmund claimed that the threats were merely a joke. However, Ressler opted not to go for an interview again while being alone. According to Douglas and Ressler, they concluded that among all the interviews they conducted in various prisons, Edmund proved to be the most intelligent prisoner ever interviewed.

Douglas described Kemper as a prisoner who liked to talk. He had a high degree of self-awareness, and because they had all the information about his crime, they were in a position to detect a lie from him. Edmund composed himself and said the truth. Once asked about his mother, he was emotionally moved and claimed that his mother molested him and made him sleep in the basement, the reason being that he might molest his sister. Due to these treatments, his hate for women grew even more rapidly. This made him feel angry and dangerous, and he killed all the cats in their family. As time went by, that feeling of hatred of women continued to grow. Though he continued to live with his mother, he said that he hated her the most.

The most interesting thing that puzzled Douglas was the way Edmund considered his killing as a game. He crafted ways and tactics to make the girls feel very comfortable around him. This made them feel at ease and he later killed them. His ultimate goal was to kill his mother, and as he told Douglas, he would quietly walk into his mother's room as she slept and envision hitting her with a hammer before he went out to kill other girls.

Other Books By RJ Parker

Experience a thought-provoking and engrossing read with books from RJ Parker Publishing. Featuring the work of crime writer and publisher RJ Parker, as well as many other authors, our company features exciting True CRIME and CRIME Fiction books in eBook, Paperback, and Audiobook editions.

rjpp.ca/RJ-PARKER-BOOKS

Serial Killers Encyclopedia

The ultimate reference for anyone compelled by the pathology and twisted minds behind the most disturbing of homicidal monsters. From A to Z, and from around the world, these serial killers have killed in excess of 3,000 innocent victims, affecting thousands of friends and family members. There are monsters in this book that you may not have heard of, but you won't forget them after reading their case. This reference book will make a great addition to a collection for true crime aficionados.

WARNING: *There are 15 dramatic crime scene photos in this book that some may find extremely disturbing*

Amazon Links- *eBook | Paperback | Audiobook*

Parents Who Killed Their Children: Filicide

This collection of "Filicidal Killers" provides a gripping overview of how things can go horribly wrong in once-loving families. Parents Who Killed their Children depicts ten of the most notorious and horrific cases of homicidal parental units out of control. People like Andrea Yates, Diane Downs, Susan Smith, and Jeffrey MacDonald received a great deal of media attention. The author explores the reasons, from addiction to postpartum psychosis, insanity to altruism, revenge and jealousy. Each story is detailed with background information on the parents, the murder scenes, trials, sentencing and aftermath.

SUSPENSE MAGAZINE - *"Parents Who Kill Their Children is a great read for aficionados of true crime. The way the author laid the cases out made the hair on the back of my neck stand up."*

Amazon Links- *eBook | Paperback | Audiobook*

BONUS BOOK

Revenge Killings

REVENGE KILLINGS
THE COP. THE SERIAL KILLER. THE MANHUNT

CHRIS DORNER

WANTED

BESTSELLING TRUE CRIME AUTHOR
RJ PARKER

Introduction
What Happened and Why

Dorner was a former LAPD officer and was honorably discharged as a Naval reservist before he was accused of killing four people in February of 2013. The police claimed that Dorner was the author of numerous versions of a rage-filled Facebook note that later went on to become his manifesto.

In the note, Dorner had vowed to bring unconventional and asymmetrical warfare to those in a LAPD uniform, no matter if they were on duty or not. Later, Dorner was quoted in a local LA newspaper of saying that he didn't want to hurt anyone but only wanted to clear his own name.

After his death or what people are calling his supposed death, speculations are arising as to whether Dorner really was the domestic terrorist he was being portrayed as or if he was someone much less scary.

A sincere lack of evidence is the first thing that is raising alarms with a lot of people. The only pieces of evidence that can be found are ones that would arouse speculation at best. Until now, there have been sightings of people who look like Dorner who have killed people. As well, a photo of a .308 sniper rifle and a handgun has emerged, but these weapons were not used to connect Dorner with the murders since the modus operandi was majorly different from the ones that have been portrayed.

Additionally, there are multiple versions of the 'manifesto' circulating about the incident, but they are more related to the rights that the 2nd Amendment grants a person so that they can be called a terrorist as is being portrayed in modern day media. Most of the manifesto is based around Dorner's rather desperate attempts to clear his own name and not around killing people.

Additionally, apart from someone called Ronald Quan pretending to be Dorner, there is no evidence that Dorner himself had killed Monica Quan and her fiancé Keith Lawrence.

Another reason why the internet is in an uproar is over the fact that, despite this being the biggest manhunt for a single person since 9/11, we know very little about the case. The case involved FBI, SWAT teams, the services of over 10,000 police officers as well as tightened border patrol, especially in the Big Bear, California area. Furthermore, drones, helicopters and aerial teams with heat sensing technology were used, but they finally ended up having to roast Dorner in a cabin in Big Bear.

The interesting part is that usually charred corpses can be recognized via DNA or medical records or other means, but Dorner was recognized by his driver's license that was found near his burnt corpse in the basement of the cabin. A lot of people are claiming this to be absurd since the heat was so intense that it burnt the full cabin down and took Dorner with it, and hence the chances of a plastic identification card or a driver's license of surviving are almost nonexistent.

Furthermore, elements of the operation have caused Joe Citizen to raise eyebrows as well. In his own words, CBS correspondent John Miller who is also former head of the LAPD Major Crimes Unit, stated that:

"There was a remarkable bit of pre-staging involved in the crime scene." He

said that the police were only keeping quiet in order to save and cover up the fact that they had let Dorner escape again. *"However, if Dorner really is still alive, it is interesting to note that he hasn't yet contacted the media as he was prone to do before the operation against him. Sources said that Dorner had cut off any and all electronic devices and ties he had on January 31. He realizes the fact that even the slightest bit of electronic activity would get him into trouble and would cause the authorities to come chasing after him yet again. Sources are also saying that the police is still on edge and is looking for any signs to jump on the fact that the body in the cabin was not in fact Dorner's body after all."*

Another reason for the raised suspicions is the fact that the LAPD blew the whole scenario way out of proportion.

Keeping in mind the fact that the LAPD is one of the most militarized police forces in America, one man's attempts to clear his name should not have sent the whole LAPD into the frenzy that it went into after Dorner's manifesto and statement came to light.

Los Angeles has its share of some of the world's most ruthless and well-armed crime rings. These include The Crips, Bloods, Mexican Mafia, Yakuza, Armenian Mob, Aryan Brotherhood, Skinheads, and Russian mobs as well as the local drug cartels. These gangs are not only real, they are openly hostile towards the LAPD and have killed numerous police officers on numerous occasions.

Some of these gangs have even murdered entire families with the LAPD unable to catch them. Yet when an ex-cop, wanting to clear his name, tried to speak out against the LAPD, the police goes all out, 'balls to the wall', and embarked on one of the most organized and widespread manhunts in recent history.

Additionally, newer reports regarding Monica Quan have arisen that render an even greater air of speculation to the whole ordeal. Monica Quan and her fiancé, both with law enforcement backgrounds, were found in a car that was parked in a parking garage in a million-dollar predominantly white neighborhood. The parking garage was being guarded by a police officer who did not see Dorner, a large black man, break in. Additionally, the garages are monitored 24/7 and yet there is no footage of Dorner either breaking in, killing anyone, being there or leaving. Nothing. But that's what the LAPD wants people to believe.

All these scenarios separately might not mean much, but added together, they make the whole plot look like a poorly directed movie.

***

"I've heard many officers who state they see dead victims as ATVs, Waverunners, RVs and new clothes for their kids. Why would you shed a tear for them when they in return crack a smile for your loss because of the impending extra money they will receive in their next paycheck for sitting at your loved ones crime scene of 6 hours because of the overtime they will accrue. They take photos of your loved ones recently deceased bodies with their cellphones and play a game of who has the most graphic dead body of the night with

officers from other divisions." [1]

In his manifesto, Christopher Dorner claimed that police officers had no compassion for the citizens they owed so much to. He alleged that the police were so desensitized that they did not care for the victims, instead disrespecting them by taking photos of gruesome crime scenes only to compare them later. He claimed that police officers didn't care about victims because they got paid overtime just to appear and remain at the crime scene.

"I never had the opportunity to have a family of my own, I'm terminating yours. Quan, Anderson, Evans, and BOR members look your wives/husbands and surviving children directly in the face and tell them the truth as to why your children are dead."

Dorner openly threatened the board that reviewed and investigated his case against Teresa Evans. Interestingly, he also suspected his own union representative Randal Quan of some sort of misconduct as well since he included him on the hit-list too.

Background

Christopher Jordan Dorner was born on June 4, 1979 in New York, although he spent most of his childhood on the west coast in the South Californian Counties of Los Angeles and Orange County. Dorner stated, later on in his life, that he was the only African American student in his school from grades one through six and that he had gotten into multiple scuffles over his race.

He attended John F. Kennedy School in La Palma and Cypress High School in Cypress where he graduated in 1997. He went on to study Political Science (major) with a minor in Psychology. He subsequently graduated from Southern Utah University in 2001.

When he was a teenager, Dorner had already made the decision to become a police officer and embarked on his journey to do so by enrolling in a youth program offered by the La Palma Police Department.

It is worth noting that, at the time when the shootings occurred (the focus of this book), Dorner himself lived in La Palma. His neighbors described him as a son of an admired and amiable family though he usually kept to himself. Dorner was not married at the time of the shootings though he had been so previously. Court records state that his wife had filed for divorce early on in 2007. [2]

***

Christopher Dorner worked as a United States Navy Reserve Officer and was honorably discharged as a lieutenant in 2013. Commissioned in 2002, Dorner was commander of a Naval Security Unit at the Naval Air Station Fallon, Nevada.

Dorner also served with the Mobile Inshore Undersea Warfare Unit from June 2004 to February 2006. He was deployed to Bahrain with the Coastal Riverine Group Two from November 2006 to April 2007. He was discharged from the United States Naval Reserve in February of 2013.

Dorner joined the LAPD during his time serving at the Naval Reserve. He entered the academy in 2005 and graduated a year later in 2006. He started serving as a probationary police officer, but his duties were interrupted shortly after he started as he was deployed to Bahrain. Records show that on his return from Naval Reserve duty in July 2007, he was partnered with his LAPD training officer, Teresa Evans, in order to complete his probationary duty. According to the Los Angeles Times, Evans later stated that even on his first day working with her, Dorner had told her that he planned to sue the LAPD as soon as he had completed his probationary duties.

On July 28 of the same year, Dorner and Evans responded to reports of a disturbance that had taken place in the Doubletree Hotel in San Pedro where they found a disturbance being caused by a man named Christopher Gettler who suffered from dementia and schizophrenia. It was Gettler's arrest that marked the start of red notes appearing in Dorner's personnel file. After the arrest, Evans conducted a performance review of Dorner which indicated that he needed to improve in several areas. Immediately after this,

Dorner filed a report stating that Evans had used excessive force in her handling of Gettler.

Dorner accused Evans of kicking Gettler in the face twice despite him being handcuffed and lying on the ground and therefore did not present any threat and hadn't resisted arrest.

This report caused the LAPD to launch an investigation that examined the report filed against Evans. The LAPD internal review board consisted of two LAPD captains as well as a criminal defense attorney. The investigation lasted seven months, during which Teresa Evans was assigned to desk duty and was forbidden to earn any money outside of her LAPD job. Dorner's representative attorney at the board hearing was a former LAPD captain named Randal Quan.

The review board was very thorough in its investigation and heard testimony from a good number of witnesses. These included three hotel employees who testified that they had witnessed most of the incident and had not seen the training officer manhandle the man, let alone kick him in any way.

Though Gettler had been brought in and had been treated for facial injuries post-arrest, he did not immediately mention being kicked in the face. However, later that day when Gettler was handed over to his father, he claimed that he had been kicked by an officer, a fact that his father testified to later at Dorner's disciplinary hearing.

In a videotaped interview with Dorner's attorney, Gettler said that he had been kicked in the face by a female police officer at the mentioned time and place. But when he was called to testify at the hearing, his replies to the board's questions are said to be noted as generally incoherent and non-responsive. The board concluded the investigation on the basis that there had been no kicking or excessive use of force and that Dorner had lied.

***

After the investigation, Dorner was fired by the LAPD due to making false accusations in his report as well as in his testimony against his training officer Teresa Evans. [3]

Dorner's attorney, Randal Quan, later stated that Dorner had been treated unfairly and had been used as a scapegoat just to protect the wrongdoings of a training officer.

Dorner later appealed his termination from the LAPD Board of Rights by filing a '*Writ of Mandamus*' with the Los Angeles County Supreme Court. The verdict was interesting, to say the least, as Judge David Yaffe wrote that he wasn't sure whether the training officer had actually kicked the suspect or not. However, he chose to uphold the department's decision regarding Dorner. Yaffe ruled that even though he himself was not certain whether Dorner's report regarding training Officer Evans was accurate or not, the LAPD board's investigation would hold merit and he, Yaffe, would be passing a verdict based on that.

This caused Dorner to actually cry out during the court proceedings in disbelief and he was recorded to have exclaimed, '*I was telling the truth! How could this happen?*' These words were later found to be repeated in Dorner's manifesto.

After this ruling, Dorner appealed to

the California Court of Appeal to the Second Appellate District. The higher court upheld the lower court's ruling and affirmed it on October 3, 2011. According to California law, the administrative findings are entitled to be presumed as correct and the petitioner is supposed to bear the burden of proving that they are incorrect since Dorner could not provide substantial evidence.

Thus, the court ruled that the LAPD board of rights had passed the correct decision and its findings were true that Dorner had not been credible in his allegations against training officer Teresa Evans.

When his fellow colleagues were interviewed, many of them had only nice things to say about Dorner. Even though a lot of people claimed that they had never been especially close to Dorner, they said that he was a great person who put his morals and good nature above all else. They claimed that there was seldom a moment when Dorner had not been seen smiling.

However, a few other colleagues had less than polite things to say about Dorner. Some officers stated that Dorner had been one to use his race as leverage to pick fights, but there are no records of any fights being recorded involving Dorner, let alone fights that Dorner himself might have initiated.

The Dorner Manifesto

It was early in February 2013 when Dorner posted a detailed note on his Facebook profile. This note coincided with what was only the start of a series of revenge shootings. In this note, Dorner discussed his history, his motivations, as well as his plans for the future. The note was around 11,000 words long and it became known later as the 'Dorner Manifesto'. [4]

Dorner's manifesto contained a list of around forty law enforcement personnel who he wanted to kill. Dorner stated that he knew that most of the people who know him personally would be in a state of shock and disbelief to hear that he was the suspect of committing such horrendous murders and having taken such drastic measures in the past few days.

However, he claimed that unfortunately he had been forced to act as what he described as the 'necessary evil' that he didn't enjoy but must partake in and complete for a substantial change to arise in the LAPD as well as in order to clear his name. He claimed that the department, far from getting better or changing since the '*Rampart Scandal*' and '*Rodney King*' days, had only gotten worse.

Dorner had just one demand: a public declaration by the LAPD that they had terminated him 'unfairly' simply because he had raised his voice and reported the use of excessive force. He urged journalists to pursue the 'fine truth' by pointing out some specific points from the investigation for reporters to follow under the Freedom of Information Act. He also claimed that he had dispatched video evidence to multiple news agencies.

On February 9, 2013, in response to Dorner's manifesto and the start of a murderous spree, LAPD Chief Charlie Beck assured Dorner through media that there would be a review of his case and the hearings that led to his dismissal. He assured Dorner that a full investigation would be launched by officials and his claims that his career was sabotaged by racist colleagues would be thoroughly examined.

Key Points Of The Manifesto

The manifesto was more an account of the happenings that had led him to the point where he thought that violence was his only option. The note contained some accounts of racial behavior toward Dorner that he had faced in his time working for different forces at different levels. [5]

In it, Dorner accused the LAPD of twisting facts when it came to his case against Training Officer Teresa Evans, the final straw that led to his termination. The following are some excerpts from this 11,000 word note:

"Even with the multiple conversations and ambient noise I heard Officer Magana call an indivdual(sic) a nigger again. Now that I had confirmed it, I told Magana not to use that word again. I explained that it was a well known offensive word that should not be used by anyone. He replied, 'I'll say it when I want'." Officer Burdios, a friend of his, also stated that he would say 'nigger' when he wanted and never gave the word another

thought.

"At that point I jumped over my front passenger seat and two other officers, then placed my hands around Burdios' neck and squeezed. I stated to Burdios don't fucking say that. At that point there was pushing and shoving and we were separated by several other officers. What I should have done, was put a Winchester Ranger SXT 9mm 147 grain bullet in his skull and Officer Magana's skull. The Situation would have been resolved effective, immediately."

This is the first sign in the manifesto where Dorner raises a point about officers using racial slurs that were offensive to him. He further pointed out that the officers continued to defiantly use the terms time and time again and even 'ganged up' against Dorner to ridicule him, a situation that only led him to violent acts.

In his manifesto, Dorner doesn't seem to be grieving over the fact that he reacted heatedly to the situation. Instead, he seemed sorry that he had not taken Officers Magana and Burdios's lives on the spot.

"The LAPD's actions have cost me my law enforcement career that began on 2/7/05 and ended on 1/2/09. They cost me my Naval career which started on 4/02 and ends on 2/13."

Dorner stated that it was the LAPD's actions that ended his short-lived career as a law enforcement official as well as his naval career. *"I've lost everything because the LAPD took my name and new [sic] I was INNOCENT!!! Capt Phil Tingirides, Justin Eisenberg, Martella, Randy Quan, and Sgt. Anderson all new [sic] I was innocent but decided to terminate me so they could continue Ofcr. Teresa Evans career. I know about the meeting between all of you where Evans attorney, Rico, confessed that she kicked Christopher Gettler (excessive force). Your day has come."*

Dorner also stated that he had lost everything he had because the LAPD had ruined his name despite the fact that he had been innocent. He went on, saying that the members of the investigative board were all aware that he was innocent but due to their desire to keep officer Teresa Evans's career intact, they acted against Dorner. He went so far as to say that Evans's attorney had confessed that she had kicked Gettler in the face but had chosen not to act upon that information.

"I'm not an aspiring rapper, I'm not a gang member, I'm not a dope dealer, I don't have multiple babies momma's. I am an American by choice, I am a son, I am a brother, I am a military service member, I am a man who has lost complete faith in the system, when the system betrayed, slandered, and libeled me. I lived a good life and though not a religious man I always stuck to my own personal code of ethics, ethos and always stuck to my shoreline and true North. I didn't need the US Navy to instill Honor, Courage, and Commitment in me but I thank them for re-enforcing it. It's in my DNA."

Here, Dorner allegedly claimed that he was being treated unfairly due to racial stereotypes. Dorner can be seen emphasizing the fact that he does not fit the stereotype that most people seem to have about dark-skinned people. He stated that he had always been a man of good judgment who valued his own code of ethics above all else and that the Navy hadn't drilled these values into his system but had only reinforced them.

"Self Preservation is no longer important to me. I do not fear death as I died long ago on 1/2/09. I was told by my mother that sometimes bad things happen to good people. I refuse to accept that."

It seems that long ago, before he tried to pin his thoughts down, Dorner had accepted the fact that his mission was a suicidal one. However, even knowing that no good would possibly come out of his plans, Dorner decided to go through with said arrangements in an attempt to fight back against fate and possibly the system in hopes of clearing his name and redeeming himself somehow.

"From 2/05 to 1/09 I saw some of the most vile things humans can inflict on others as a police officer in Los Angeles. Unfortunately, it wasn't in the streets of LA. It was in the confounds [sic] of LAPD police stations and shops (cruisers). The enemy combatants in LA are not the citizens and suspects, it's the police officers."

Again, we see hints of Dorner's

allegations against the entirety of the LAPD of misdemeanors, especially treating the people they were supposed to be helping unfairly. He emphasized time and time again how the police were misusing and abusing their powers and targeting the people they should have been helping in the first place.

Time and time again in the manifesto, Dorner stated that all it would take for him to stop the killings would be for the LAPD to tell the people what the truth was and to clear his name from the false accusations that had been used against him.

"This department has not changed from the Daryl Gates and Mark Fuhrman days. Those officers are still employed and have all been promoted to Command staff and supervisory positions. I will correct this error. Are you aware that an officer (a rookie/probationer at the time) seen on the Rodney King videotape striking Mr. King multiple times with a baton on 3/3/91 is still employed by the LAPD and is now a Captain on the police department? Captain Rolando Solano is now the commanding officer of a LAPD

police station (West LA division). As a commanding officer, he is now responsible for over 200 officers. Do you trust him to enforce department policy and investigate use of force investigations on arrestees by his officers? Are you aware Evans has since been promoted to Sergeant after kicking Mr. Gettler in the face. Oh, you violated a citizens civil rights? We will promote you."

Dorner claimed that instead of dealing swift and crisp justice to the people who abuse their powers, the LAPD instead rewards them. He quoted multiple counts and cases where the officers who had been known to misuse and abuse their powers had been rewarded greatly for their misconduct instead of having been reprimanded and punished like they should have been. Quoting his own case, Dorner stated that as a reward for kicking Gettler in the face, training officer Teresa Evans had been promoted to the level of Sergeant. He claimed that even the officers who had video evidence against them of hitting, injuring and using excessive force against suspects had not only been let go free but had also been promoted to positions of great power with some of them being put in charge of hundreds of other officers. Dorner questioned what sort of a police force these officers who were excessively violent themselves would train for the near future.

"Those lesbian officers in supervising positions who go to work, day in day out, with the sole intent of attempting to prove your misandrist authority (not feminism) to degrade male officers. You are a high value target."

Dorner started hinting at and naming victims blatantly throughout his manifesto. He claimed that racism wasn't the only problem with the police force. Female officers with a modicum of power used their power to commit acts of misandry against male officers. He claimed that anyone who freely abused their power was rewarded.

"Those of you who "go along to get along" have no backbone and destroy the foundation of courage. You are the enablers of those who are guilty of misconduct. You are just as guilty as those who break the code of ethics and oath you swore."

Dorner believed that the people who were unwilling to fight against the system and the misconduct and the abuse of powers by those above, below and around them had breached the code of ethics and the oath they had taken. In his eyes, they seem to be just as guilty as the abusers.

"I've heard many officers who state they see dead victims as ATVs, Waverunners, RVs and new clothes for their kids. Why would you shed a tear for them when they in return crack a smile for your loss because of the impending extra money they will receive in their next paycheck for sitting at your loved ones crime scene of 6 hours because of the overtime they will accrue. They take photos of your loved ones recently deceased bodies with their cellphones and play a game of who has the most graphic dead body of the night with officers from other divisions."

In his manifesto, Dorner claimed that police officers had no compassion for the citizens they owed so much to. He alleged that the police were so desensitized that they did not care for the victims, instead disrespecting them by taking photos of gruesome crime scenes only to compare them later. He claimed that police officers didn't care about victims because they got paid overtime just to appear and remain at the crime scene.

"I never had the opportunity to have a family of my own, I'm terminating yours. Quan, Anderson, Evans, and BOR members Look your wives/husbands and surviving children directly in the face and tell them the truth as to why your children are dead."

Dorner openly threatened the board that reviewed his case and investigated his case against Evans. Interestingly, he also suspected his own representative Randal Quan of some sort of misconduct as well since he included him on the hit-list too. Another member of the list happened, typically, to be Teresa Evans.

"You said that I should have kept my mouth shut about another officer's misconduct. Maybe you were right. But I'm not built like others, it's not in my DNA and my history has always shown that. When you view the video of the suspect stating he was kicked by Evans, maybe you will see that I was a decent person

after all. I told the truth."

Dorner alleged that he had been told to keep quiet about the misconduct demeanor by his training officer Teresa Evans. He said that it was against his morals to twist the truth and pretend he had not seen what he had just to protect his own skin and his training officer.

Dorner's manifesto was a sort of action plan stating what he was going to do to the police officers. In various online postings, Dorner taunted Randal Quan after murdering his 28-year-old daughter Monica Quan. Allegedly, Dorner even called Quan in order to gloat over his daughter's death.

Dorner wrote in online postings that if anyone is to be blamed for the deaths, it is the culprits who ruined his career, are using the LAPD as a headquarters for their tyranny and are providing injustice in the name of justice. He said that if anyone was to be blamed for Monica Quan's death, it should be her father Randal Quan himself.

According to reports, a man claiming to be Christopher Dorner called Quan shortly after Monica's death had taken place but before her body had been discovered. Reports state that the man told Quan that he should have done a better job of protecting his own daughter. Shortly after this, the LAPD publicly pushed for Dorner to hand himself in for the first time. This appeal was accompanied by a $1 million bounty for anyone who had any leads as to where Dorner was hiding.

LAPD Chief Charlie Beck said that, though the $1 million bounty had probably been one of the biggest ever offered in Southern California, it was remarkably easy to secure due to the fact that Dorner was proving to be such a security threat to law enforcement officials and their families in the region. A huge sum of the reward was raised by local police officers, businesses, communities as well as local governments across Southern California.

In a press conference held not long after the reward was announced, Los Angeles Mayor Antonio Villaraigosa announced that he would do all in his power to stop Dorner's 'reign of terror'.

When asked if he would approve the usage of 'drones' as had been used around the world in the 'war on terror', the mayor gave a very cryptic reply of, '*the police would be using all tools at their disposal in order to capture Dorner.*'

It is interesting to note that in his manifesto, Dorner had clearly stated that he had no qualms in coming in quietly, if only the LAPD would release the truth and, especially, release the video interview of Christopher Gettler in which he is clearly stating that he was kicked in the face by a female police officer, who was training officer Teresa Evans.

However, it seemed that the LAPD had no desire to capture Dorner alive as was later established by the fact that on no less than two separate occasions, the police had opened fire on two passing cars simply because they fit the profile of the vehicle Dorner was supposed to have been driving.

In two separate incidents that took place in the early morning hours on February, 7, 2013, police opened fire on people who later turned out to be unrelated to Christopher Dorner in any way. Dorner was not even present at either scene when the shootings occurred.

The first incident took place at

around 6:00 a.m. where at least seven LAPD officers, who were assigned to the protection of an unnamed LAPD official's residence in the Los Angeles County city of Torrance, opened fire at a passing light blue Toyota Tacoma.

There were two Hispanic occupants inside the car, Emma Hernandez, 71 and her daughter Margie Carranza, 47. The mother and daughter were delivering newspapers for the LA Times. Their vehicle, according to the police officers who had opened fire, was heading towards the home they were protecting, and had matched the description of Dorner's grey Nissan Titan and was moving without its headlights on.

Emma was shot in the back while Carranza suffered injuries to her hand. The attorney representing the women later stated that the police had no idea who was inside the vehicle. He said that there was nothing about his clients that remotely matched Dorner's profile, nor were their trucks even remotely similar. The two injured women later testified that the police had given them no warning prior to opening fire on their vehicle.

Further investigations revealed that

the police had questioned Carranza's neighbors who stated that the two ladies delivered newspapers every single morning and that they always kept the headlights off so as to not disturb the neighbors in their sleep.

Later, the LAPD launched an internal investigation into the matter. The attorney for Hernandez and Carranza stated that their truck was riddled with 102 bullet holes.

Author's note: this clearly establishes the fact that the rules of engagement were to kill Dorner. I don't believe the LAPD had any intentions of taking him alive. My opinion will further be supported during the manhunt and cabin fire.

The LAPD has refused to comment on how many bullets were fired, how many holes were found, as well as how many police officers had been involved in shooting at the truck. It is also not mentioned if the two women were given any sort of verbal warning before firepower was opened up on them.

Later that year in April, the police

paid a $4.2 million settlement to Emma Hernandez and Margie Carranza, the two ladies who had suffered from bullet wounds at the hands of the police on the morning of February 7.

On the same day, less than half an hour after this incident took place, officers from the Torrance Police Department opened fire on yet another vehicle.

As in the first incident, officers involved in this shooting claimed that they had opened fire due to the similar resemblance of the vehicle in question to that of Christopher Dorner's truck. But later the vehicle was discovered to be a black Honda Ridgeline and the driver was found to be a white male.

The victim was David Perdue who was simply on his way to the beach in order to surf for a while before he went to work.

A Torrance Police Department cruiser smashed into Perdue's pickup before they opened fire on the vehicle. Fortunately, Perdue was not struck by any of the bullets. But he did suffer multiple injuries from the impact against his truck. The police later claimed that they had acted upon the similarities between the Perdue's and Dorner's vehicles. It was later confirmed by law enforcement that the vehicle was a different make and color than that of Dorner's.

A year after these incidents took place, on February 4, 2014, it was determined by the LAPD chief Charlie Beck that the police officers had indeed used extensive and excessive force against the two women and Mr. Purdue. He said that the eight officers involved had violated the LAPD's use of force policy and that disciplinary action was being taken against them. California state law prevented him from disclosing the nature of the corrective action but that the punishment could range from extended retraining up to termination. However, no criminal charges had been laid against any of these officers.

It is interesting to note that not long after these civilians had been shot at, online protest forums against the LAPD had popped up stating that they had great apprehensions against how Dorner were dismissed from the police service.

Furthermore, they had protested against how the police had a license to kill anyone they so pleased just because they thought that the victim looked like the suspect they had been pursuing.

Time line

There are key events that took place during the Christopher Dorner debacle - the fired LAPD police officer who was suspected of having killed three people including a fellow police officer in Southern Carolina.

Dorner was said to have been working on his manifesto in which he had outlined plans to kill the police officers and their families who had, in some way or another wronged him, as well as their families.

- **Sunday, February 3** - assistant women's college basketball coach Monica Quan, 28, and her fiancé Keith Lawrence, 27, were found shot to death in a parked car in Irvine, California outside their condominium. Monica was the daughter of the former LAPD Captain and lawyer Randal Quan who represented Dorner as an attorney in his case against then training officer,

Teresa Evans, in front of an Internal Review Board who then fired Dorner.

- Dorner called Randal Quan shortly after shooting his daughter and taunted him for not providing his daughter with better protection.

- **Monday, February 4** - some of Dorner's belongings as well as his police equipment were found in a trashcan in San Diego near the Irvine crime scene, thus linking him to the killings of Monica and Keith.

- **Wednesday, February 6** - the police first found Dorner's manifesto online, and he became suspect number one.

- A man matching Dorner's description made an attempt to steal a boat from a San Diego marina. The attempt was a failed one. An 81-year-old man was found tied up on the vessel that was meant to have been stolen, but otherwise he was unharmed.

- **Thursday, February** 7 - around 1:30 am LAPD officers who were protecting an unknown person named in the manifesto chased a vehicle they believed was Dorner's. During the pursuit, one police officer was grazed in the forehead by a bullet but remained otherwise unscathed. The gunman escaped unidentified from the premises.

- On the same date a few hours later, a shooter believed to be Dorner ambushed two Riverside Police Officers who were doing a routine patrol. After a brief struggle, one officer lost his life whilst another was critically injured. Dorner escaped yet again.

- Again on the same date around 2:20 pm, a bus driver from a shuttle bus turned in a wallet with an LAPD badge and the picture identification of Christopher Dorner to the San Diego Police. The wallet was found less than five miles from the boat near the San Diego International Airport.

- 5:30 am on February 7, eight LAPD officers guarding another unknown manifesto target in the Los Angeles suburb of Torrance opened fire on a truck they believed to have belonged to Christopher Dorner. It was later found out that the truck was not even the same make and model as the one which Dorner drove. The occupants were a mother and daughter who were delivering newspapers. Both suffered gunshot wounds with the mother suffering a wound to her back and the daughter getting injured in the hand.

- Not long after the incident above, on the same date, the LAPD again opened fire and slammed a cruiser into another truck they believed to be similar to that of Dorner's. The passenger in the truck suffered minor injuries from impact but was not hurt otherwise.

- At 8:35 am, the police found a burnt-out pickup truck near the Big Bear ski area in the San Bernardino Mountains. The truck was examined and the authorities confirmed a few hours later that it was indeed Dorner's truck.

- At 9:40 am, the Naval Base Point Loma in San Diego was locked down after some Navy workers reported seeing someone who resembled Christopher Dorner. Military officials later confirmed that Dorner had indeed checked into a hotel on the base earlier in the week, on a Tuesday, but had checked out shortly after on Wednesday. Dorner used a military ID to check in.

- Just after 4:00 pm the same day, authorities searched a Las Vegas-area home that was said to have belonged to Dorner. They left with several boxes of items. The authorities later stated that no weapons had been found at the premises, but they still declined to comment as to what was discovered and taken away in the boxes.

- **Friday February 8**, dozens of searchers set out to hunt for Dorner in the freezing, snowy mountains of San Bernardino after they lost his

175

footprints near the site where the truck had been found. Authorities had also searched Dorner's mother's house where they had collected ten bags of evidence and had also taken multiple electronic items for examination. The police also searched a storage locker in Buena Park.

- **Saturday February 9**, police helicopters used heat-seeking technology to search for Dorner in the mountains near Big Bear. Authorities later revealed that weapons and camping equipment was found in Dorner's burnt truck.

- **Sunday February 10**, the authorities announced a $1 million reward for any information leading to Dorner's arrest.

- **Monday February 11**, Riverside County Prosecutors issued a warrant charging Dorner with murdering a police officer and attempting to murder three other police officers in a case which punishment could potentially be a death penalty. Authorities had received more than

176

700 tips for Dorner's whereabouts since the reward had been announced.

- **Tuesday February 12**, police were alerted to a call after a man fitting Dorner's profile stole a vehicle in the San Bernardino Mountains. The vehicle was found rather quickly on Highway 38. After being found out, the suspect ran into the forest and barricaded himself inside a cabin.

- Twenty minutes later, the State Fish and Wildlife wardens were involved in a shoot-out with the suspect. During the cross-fire, two San Bernardino County Sheriff's deputies were wounded.

- Four hours later, police surrounded the cabin from all sides where the suspect was holed up. Gunfire erupted before the entire cabin caught on fire and law enforcement officials decided to wait for the fire to burn itself out.

- About thirty minutes later, a San Bernardino County Sheriff's spokeswoman confirmed that one of

177

the two wounded deputies had died and the other was in surgery and was expected to survive.

The saga ended later that night around 6:30 pm when the police found a charred body in the rubble of the burnt cabin. Though they refrained from confirming the identity at the time, the police later confirmed that the body did indeed belong to Christopher Dorner.

Inquiry

Shortly before Christopher Dorner's death on February 12, LAPD Chief Charlie Beck assured the public that they would reopen Dorner's case that led to his termination. He said that the purpose behind this was not to appease a murderer but in fact to reassure the public that the police department is transparent and fair in all that it does.

Numerous experts believed this to be a measure of damage control taken by the Chief of Police in order to avoid another riot like the ones that occurred in 1992 where people caused an uproar upon the emergence of a video tape showing white police officers beating a black man called Rodney King.

In explaining why he chose to reopen Dorner's case, the LAPD chief said *"The LAPD has made tremendous strides in gaining the trust and confidence of the people we serve."* He added, *"Dorner's actions may cause a pause in our increasingly positive relationship with the*

179

community."

To reiterate, Dorner joined the LAPD in 2005 and was fired in 2008 for giving false statements against his training officer Teresa Evans. He later went on to sue the department and lost the case as well as the appeal he made against it.

This decision to reopen the case was a significant turn-around from the stance the chief of police had shown a mere few days ago when he said that a trial or retrial simply wasn't possible. In his own words, when asked about the possibility of reopening the case, the chief commented, *"You're talking about a homicide suspect who has committed atrocious crimes."* He further added, *"If you want to give any attribution to his ramblings on the Internet, go right ahead. But I do not."*

When asked about Dorner's attempts to clear his name and set the records straight, the chief said that that simply was not going to happen.

The history of the LAPD has been especially fraught with tensions between the police force and the African American community both inside and outside the

LAPD. Multiple times, people working inside the LAPD have insisted that racial discrimination was more than uncommon.

This coupled with the fact that shortly after Dorner's manifesto came to surface, the police opened fire on a car containing two Hispanic women raised a lot of alarms for everyone within the LAPD as people began to speculate whether the department simply made a lot of mistakes, or whether it really was as racially biased as they had been led to believe time and time again.

WARNING: Some photos may be disturbing

Photos

IMAGE 1

U.S. Reservist Chris Dorner

IMAGE 2

Dorner and Former LAPD Chief Wm. Bratton

IMAGE 3

*Monica Quan, 28, the daughter of LAPD Captain
Randal Quan and her fiance Keith Lawrence, 27*

IMAGE 4

*Riverside Police Officer Michael Crain gunned
down by Dorner on Feb 7, 2013*

IMAGE 5

Funeral of Officer Michael Crain

IMAGE 6

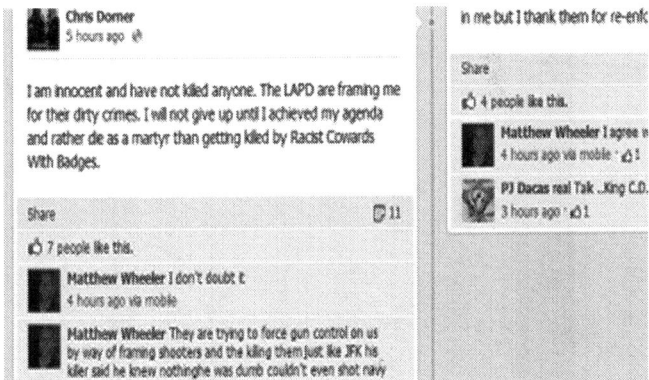

A Facebook post from Dorner claiming his innocence

IMAGE 7

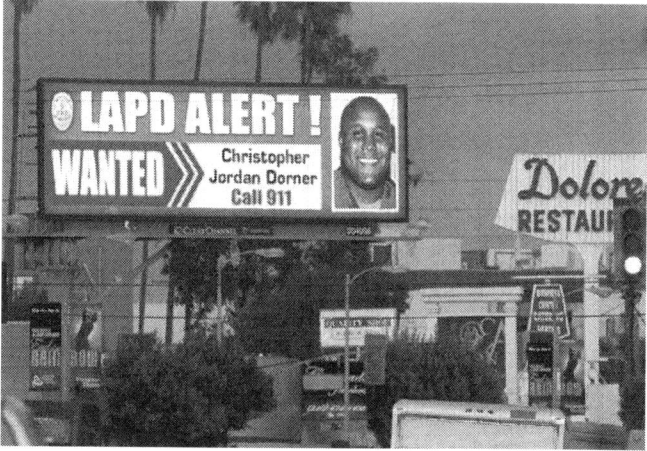

Digital billboard LAPD Alert during the manhunt

IMAGE 8

San Bernardino Detective Jeremiah MacKay killed by Dorner on Feb 12, 2013

IMAGE 9

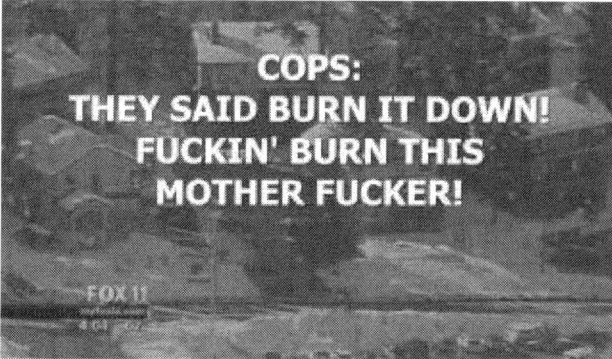

Live video and audio by FOX 11

Cops saying repeatedly to Fuckin' Burn This Mother Fucker, and Burn it Down.

Click to watch and listen

http://clipshq.me/watch/FuyiffP-7vM

IMAGE 10

*Cabin in Big Bear, California on fire where Dorner
was holed up inside*

IMAGE 11

The cabin ruins after the fire

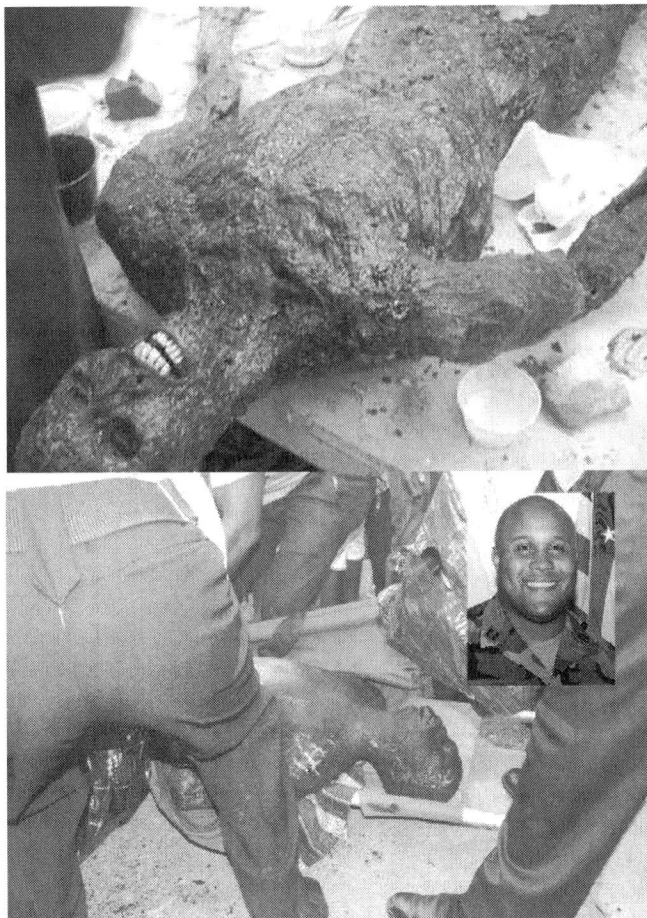

The supposed charred body of Dorner

IMAGE 13

Dorner's burnt-out truck at Big Bear

Mother and daughter's truck riddled with bullets

IMAGE 15

Another innocent citizen, rammed off the road and shot at by police

What's Next for the LAPD?

The massive manhunt for former police officer Christopher J Dorner ended in a hail of bullets and a wall of flame as the mountain cabin he'd been hiding in caught fire after a brief cross-fire with the police. Two days later, the authorities confirmed that the body that had been recovered from the wreckage had belonged to Dorner.

"The charred human remains located in the burned out cabin in Seven Oaks have been positively identified to be that of Christopher Dorner," the San Bernardino County Sheriff-Coroner's Office said in a written statement. *"During the autopsy, positive identification was made through dental examination."*

While Dorner's rampage is thankfully over, the repercussions for his actions have started to arise, and they are affecting the LAPD to the core as old animosities between the Department and the community it serves have started to rear their head.

The claims made by Dorner were bold and rather plain. In the 11,000 word manifesto he allegedly published on his Facebook page (though there are multiple accounts of the same manifesto now circulating the internet), Dorner stated that he had been discriminated against and had been deliberately driven out of the department for the simple crime of speaking up against the misconduct as he witnessed it committed by his training officer Teresa Evans.

He accused Evans of kicking a docile and bound suspect in the face twice. Issues of race and police brutality in relation with black people are not uncommon. Los Angeles is the city where the videotape of the police brutally beating black motorcyclist Rodney King first arose. What's more, the officers accused of beating the black man on video tape were later acquitted. This case caused multiple riots in 1992. The Department was also immersed in a flood of corruption charges and civil rights violations which later went on to be known as the Rampart Scandal. [6]

This scandal went on for the duration of the late 90s as well as the early 2000s.

Eventually, this situation calmed down somewhat when the LAPD and the federal government sent an independent monitor to guide and enforce reforms.

Dorner stated in his manifesto that the situation had not changed a bit from the Rampart and Rodney King days but had in fact only gotten worse.

Dorner's words and the actions that followed from both sides poured a lot of salt in the wounds that had not healed completely in the black community of Los Angeles and had caused much damage to the Department's reputation already. The LAPD has a very long history of mistreating black people.

It wasn't until as late as the 1960s before the LAPD ended the forced segregation of squad cars. Now, Dorner's accusations have revived some not-so-savory ghosts who hadn't completely died out in the first place.

Experts state that on such a massive scale as this problem had been dealt with, there are bound to be aftershocks for many years to come.

A significant cause for alarm was the

fact that callers on a local radio station that is popular in the African American community had been calling in on air and had been referring to Dorner as a hero, to the point that they even claimed that he would seek vengeance for the centuries worth of slavery that had been imposed on the black community. Furthermore, a Facebook page by the name of '*We Stand With Christopher Dorner*' had attracted more than 23,000 followers.

Dorner's supporters seem to have ignored the fact that he was supposedly a violent criminal because they see his rants not as the ravings of a lunatic but those of a man who had been oppressed by the system to the point that he set out to claim justice the only way he knew how: through force.

Though Dorner's approach to getting justice was wrong, it cannot be denied that the people who committed such racial atrocities against him, against innocent black men, against innocent and docile suspects are not any more right than the path Dorner chose. It makes a lot of people think that if this is the only way to get justice, just how old and bygone are the days old and gone by?

In an attempt to counter Dorner's resentments, the LAPD chief Charlie Beck announced that he had reopened Dorner's case. Beck stated that as hard as it had been to change the culture of the LAPD, it had been even harder to claim and maintain an air of trust inside the LAPD and between the LAPD and the public, and he would take every measure possible to maintain the air.

Therefore, Beck had continued, it is felt that the issue that has been brought to the public must be resolved in public as well. He said that this was the time to assure people that the LAPD was free and fair in all that it did. He said that he was not taking any steps to appease a murderer but to make sure that the public realized that no matter what anyone said, the police office was free and fair in all things it did.

The inquest is being taken as a sign that, despite whatever Dorner has to say, the department is trying to amend its ways and put its old days behind it.

Still, despite the fact that three civilians had been shot over mistaken identity and two of them has suffered gunshot wounds, the manhunt for Dorner had been rather successful, according to the

LAPD. The huge task force that was assembled made sure that all agencies involved coordinated with each other, even though most of the agencies involved are generally not seen at such a crime scene, such as the Department of Fish and Wildlife. All resources, in short, were put to use so that there would be no chance that Dorner would be able to escape or harm anyone.

The LAPD, however, even years later is not willing to answer these questions about the possibility of a tarnished image and is still tight-lipped with the media. But in the end, even the people who might have agreed with Dorner did not agree with his message at all simply because of the fact that violence is never the correct approach to solving any problem, no matter which side it ensues from.

His explicit threats against the LAPD members and their families and even measures against some of the aforementioned were seen as barbaric acts of a lunatic.

Experts have commented time and time again that when someone goes after the families of the LAPD, it is seen as them going after the LAPD and the families of the institution, and then even the police start to take wrongful measures.

If there had ever been an opportunity for the LAPD to take measures to sort out the mess in which it currently is, it is now.

The LAPD's history has been riddled with racial crimes and especially crimes involving an excessive use of force against the suspects they have a duty to protect. This incident, especially, has set people's eyes on to the LAPD once again to see which move they will further make.

The LAPD can use this opportunity to make changes and amends in the system so that the people of Los Angeles are put at rest as well that racial discrimination in the LAPD is a thing of the past.

The Race Factor

Though it is true that Christopher Dorner is the last person on earth anyone should be idolizing, it is also true that we can no longer ignore the impact racism has on daily lives, even in high-end fields who are dedicated to stopping such crimes - the police departments.

To ignore Dorner's grievances just because of the method he chose would be quite a grave mistake. Between all the bloodshed and the diatribe, there is an opportunity here to strike while the iron is hot and take measures to lessen if not completely eradicate the racism that runs so deeply into the system.

If he had written his manifesto in the form of a testimony, he would have been offering what Critical Race Theorists would refer to as a Racial Battle Fatigue.

Racial Battle Fatigue [7] is a theory attributed to the psychological attrition that people of color face on an almost daily basis. This arises from the daily battle of deflecting racial insults, stereotypes and discrimination. It is the cumulative effect of being on guard and having to prepare responses to insults that are both subtle and overt.

This arsenal of quick wit and always being on the alert is known as self-protection from racial microaggressions and racialized aggression. RBF is mostly experienced by people of color who work in mostly 'white institutions'.

Within such institutions, people of color (non-white groups) have to deal with prejudices, discriminatory behavior and denigrating comments from people of any level and post, juniors and peers as well as seniors.

Racial microaggressions was a concept first used to describe only the sort of discriminatory behavior that people of color face in an academic institute or educational environment, but it is true and more than apparent that now the definition holds true elsewhere.

Indeed, it wouldn't be awry to say that racial microaggressions are a part of society at large. In order to understand the scope of Racial Battle Fatigue, we must first understand racial microaggressions.

Racial microaggressions are defined as:

- Subtle insults. Range from verbal insults to non-verbal insults and are directed at people of color. These are usually used automatically or unconsciously.

- Layered insults. Based on a person's race, gender, class, sexuality, language, immigration status, accent or anything that might set them apart from what the society's norm of a white person is.

- Cumulative insults. Unnecessary stress that is layered on people of color while privileging white people.

In a daily environment, racial microaggressions take place all around us. Racial microaggressions are subtle remarks that the speaker often considers a compliment.

"You are not like other people of color."

"You don't look like a person of color."

"You speak English without an accent."

"You might be a person of color but you're not *like* them."

Racial microaggressions are part of a psychological warfare that is endured by people of color in environments that are heavy on the white population.

If you're wondering where Christopher Dorner comes into this scenario, some parts of his manifesto are a page straight out of the handbook of racial microaggressions against people of color (or would be if such a handbook existed.)

If Dorner's manifesto were to be used as raw data or something other than a criminal's game plan, one would proceed by tracing and highlighting through it, the racial themes that run throughout the whole tirade. In his manifesto, Dorner refers to two high-profile cases.

These are the Rampart Scandal and the Rodney King case both of which not only illuminated the grievances that people of color had and had been talking about for years, but also validated them. Both of these cases showed corruption in the police office to be a common occurrence.

The Rampart Scandal brought forth a whole culture of misconduct and the criminally casual abuse of authority by the LAPD, which included the false planting of evidence, using excessive force, dealing narcotics, robbing banks, as well as framing suspects for their own personal gains.

The Rodney King case in which the police were exposed using excessive use of force by viciously beating an unconscious man. An amateur videotape vividly exposed police brutality and effectively blew the LAPD's reputation to smithereens. "Serving and protecting" was revealed to be a big lie as images of cruelty and pure malice at the hands of the people's so-called protectors flooded the media.

One year after the Rodney King incident took place, the officers involved in the beating were acquitted. Minutes after the news of the decision acquitting them was broadcast, the unrest began in Los Angeles in the form of riots that later became to be known as the Los Angeles riots by the popular media.

This unrest was referred to by Critical Race Scholars as the Los Angeles Uprising of 1992. This uprising resulted in 53 deaths, thousands of injuries, and more than 6,000 incidents of fire. In solidarity with their Los Angeles brethren, San Francisco, Atlanta and Las Vegas also erupted into smaller scale uprisings.

Most of the mainstream popular newspapers stated that Dorner had a seemingly illogical and rather bottomless grudge against the LAPD when they fired him in 2009. Dorner had served for three years and stated in his manifesto that he had brought his grievances up the chain of command and had made them known to the higher-ups.

His grievances had been dismissed and he had been ultimately discharged. Dorner believed that he had been the victim of an act of revenge by the LAPD for crossing the 'Blue Line' which is an unspoken decree of secrecy between police officers.

Dorner had been portrayed by an ex-FBI profiler Jim Clemente as an "injustice collector". The reason behind this was that he held tight to detailed scenarios of what had happened, when and who did what to whom, and what the outcome of each scenario was.   He kept a record of racial microaggressions against not only himself but others as well. He cited those who had been victimized by the LAPD time and time again. These people included People of Color, the elderly, immigrants, the disabled, and hence everyone who was not in a particular position of power to defend themselves.

At some times, Dorner speaks in the character of a vigilante who is emerging from the shadows of injustice to right some wrongs. However, then he quickly crosses over to the dark side where he collects dead bodies as his severance.

According to researchers, the symptoms of Racial Battle Fatigue often include but are not limited to a loss of sense of control, insomnia, rapid mood swings, high blood pressure, ulcers and other symptoms that can be noticed in patients suffering from stress.

Stress from racial microaggressions can become rather lethal when the accumulation of physiological symptoms of Racial Battle Fatigue are left untreated, are not cared for properly, or are personally dismissed as is prone to happen in an environment where racial microaggressions are treated as a normal part of life and any voice raised against them is considered to be unnecessary noise.

This is particularly problematic as the sufferer may feel haunted by the fact that he thinks that his grievances are only imaginary. This can lead him to suffer from multiple mental health issues.

It is worth noting here that there are positive ways to dealing with the type of RBF Christopher Dorner suffered from. Being an educated man, Dorner could have dealt with his grief in a more productive way such as by going public, doing an expose, writing a book or even a screenplay depicting what he underwent and the type of activities that regularly go on inside the sacred LAPD.

He could even have staged a protest or a series of the same outside said police department. However, the minute he chose to fire the first shot, Dorner made a decision. He joined the circle of abuse and went from a victim to a predator, albeit on the other side of the line. His method of taking revenge effectively wiped out all the valid reasons he had for his frustration, and in the media that is far from unprejudiced itself, he got sidelined as his violence became the story.

By acting on his own sense of vengeance, Dorner has opened our eyes and shown us how each and every one of us is susceptible to participating in the cycle of abuse. When he was a rescuer, Dorner witnessed the abuse and incidents of usage of excessive force by his fellow officers and reported them in hopes to get some justice. In his manifesto, Dorner cites multiple counts of excessive use of unchecked power.

Dorner's manifesto was very informative in the sense that he had confronted each individual group for its actions or lack of actions and had cited the incidents as well as the responsibility of each group to stop it.

Joe Jones is another former LAPD Officer and a person of color. He countered Dorner's manifesto with one of his own where he pleaded with Dorner to stop killing innocent victims.

He made it rather clear that Dorner was not the first person to come across such a situation and hence he wasn't the only one with any grievances relating to the matter.

He made an appeal to the citizens of Los Angeles, the government, the politicians and both to the honest and dishonest members of the LAPD, as well as to Dorner himself. He said that he himself had suffered for no less than eighteen years. He calls these eighteen years of psychological strain, self-doubt and torment.

Many people of color who suffer at the hands of their superiors do so in silence. At most, the suffering is discussed with a small circle of family and friends because confronting the perpetrators of racial microaggressions or even speaking up about them comes with a risk.

The first of these risks is that you will not be believed or will be told that you are not the first to suffer as such and thus should remain silent about it, the second that you will be discredited, and the third that you will be blamed for initiating something yourself.

Out of these, the most damaging, perhaps, is the option that you will be silenced by inaction. Even more, by speaking about them, silencing by inaction makes a person believe that their words do not matter and that their grievances are imaginary at best.

Manhunt – Eric Frein in Comparison with Chris Dorner

Let's discuss a rogue police murderer of this era - Eric Frein. [8] After a massive 48-day manhunt, three deputy US Marshals saw the accused cop killer 'moving through tall grass' and yet they 'could see his hands and see that he was not carrying any sort of weapons.'

Frein was taken into custody near an airport hangar without any sort of incident whatsoever. This was completely different from the Christopher Dorner manhunt which resulted in a shootout and, ultimately, Dorner's death. This situation was also different from the confrontation and detention of the jaywalker Mike Brown in Ferguson. This also was unlike the detention and capture of the "reasonably suspicious" Ezell Ford in Los Angeles.

Officers in the police force are taught that time is on their side, there is no need to rush in and that the suspect can always be waited out. Since this is a part of the official training, one could claim that this is the official protocol the LAPD and San Bernardino Sheriff had to follow after they had surrounded the cabin where Christopher Dorner had been hiding.

The question arises, why were both departments in such a hurry that they couldn't even wait a full twenty-four or even twelve hours? What was the urgency here?

It had been reported that Dorner had been spotted in different places leading up to the cabin several times during the 9-day manhunt and had escaped the authorities every time much like Eric Frein.

Why did Ferguson's police officer Darren Wilson need to confront Mike Brown in the middle of the street and why couldn't he wait until Brown had crossed over to the sidewalk?

And what was so important a topic that a gang of LAPD officers needed to talk to Ezell Ford about that they had to confront him and initiate a struggle that ultimately ended in his death? And couldn't this "talk" wait for another day or be held in another, less lethal way?

Eric Frein had been described as a

survivalist with an extensive shooting background. He was someone with a grudge against law enforcement, someone who had premeditated over the murders he had been hoping to commit.

He had been preparing for them for months, if not years, before. Frein had been named as one of the FBI's top ten most wanted criminals, and yet he was considered to be less frightening to the law enforcement officials than Dorner, Ford or even the jaywalker Brown.

It had been reported that Frein had left or abandoned an AK-47 and ammunition as well as two pipe bombs, and they had been used as bread crumbs for the pursuing officers to discover.

However, in the matter of Frein, there were no accusations of 'scaring the police', no hiding of the hands and no reaching for the waistband. Not a flash bang had been thrown and no structures had been burnt to the ground once Frein had been spotted. Reports revealed that as soon as Frein had been spotted with his guard down, he had simply been ordered to lie face down, to which he obliged, and was later handcuffed.

There are some interesting similarities between the Christopher Dorner manhunt and the Eric Frein manhunt except for the little technical detail that Dorner had been black while Frein had been white. Frein and Dorner both had given a lot of thought to their attacks.

Both had been called armed and dangerous and both were reported to be exceptionally good shooters. Both of them allegedly killed law enforcement officials in a cold-blooded and calculated manner, and yet only one of them had been told to lie face down and had been handcuffed.

Though neither Frein's nor Dorner's actions are commendable or condoned, the apparent disparity between the way police officers treat or rather 'handle' black/brown people and white people is bothering, to say the least.

Brown or black people are not mythological creatures to be feared. They are not dragons who can only be confronted and tackled in unfair ways because they somehow have some sort of advantage over a person. What was the urgency in taking down Christopher Dorner that the police had to burn a cabin to the ground?

Additionally, what were the special circumstances that precipitated the Mike Brown Shooting? What was so scary about Ezell Ford's actions? If Eric Frein can be hunted for more than forty days in relentless pursuit and can be brought down in a non-lethal way and can be captured peacefully, should that not be the norm as to how this sort of a situation should be dealt with every time around?

There might be a lot of red tape around the capture of Frein as most of the details are still yet unknown to public. However, the fact that a serial cop killer can be given the chance to come in quietly and that a black man in South Carolina can be shot when he reaches for the driver's license a patrol officer asked for is rather alarming.

A passenger in Hammond, Indiana was ordered to show his identification and was tasered and arrested when he failed to show it. The coroner in Oklahoma ruled the death of a black man a homicide after officers struggled with him in a movie theater, and yet most of the culprits of these crimes, men and women in uniforms, got fined or a light tap on the back of their hands at the most, while Frein is still alive and innocent black men are dead.

A Forensic Outlook

It would be a crass attempt at stating the obvious to say that Christopher Dorner was an extremely angry man. Mass murderers are almost always frustrated and angry to a certain degree about something.

This could be work, love, life, finances, social status, the loss of something or someone special, failure to attain grandiose fantasies, a lack of self-recognition or acceptance of self or someone else, feelings of being persecuted, rejection, childhood trauma, or anything that can have a long-term effect on someone's psychology.

And there is often a significant grain of truth in their wrath against reality. There is often a comprehensible and somewhat understandable reason to be furious about their lives. There are two distinguishing factors in the Christopher Dorner case that set it apart from other cases about mass murderers and even other cops that have gone rogue.

221

The first is the fact that Dorner was someone who had been a former police officer. He was the typical good cop gone bad who started angrily assassinating not only former colleagues but also their families. The other is the racial component where Mr. Dorner was an African-American who believed that he had been the victim of racial discrimination. Dorner believed that, in part, he had been fired due to the color of his skin.

If you take a look at the Facebook note off Dorner's profile, which later went on to become his manifesto, he alleges the LAPD of being racist, and that is not without historical precedent.

And despite the fact that this problem had been present in the system for a long time, it had still not been eradicated completely and had resulted in the sort of psychological stress and damage caused by it as we witnessed in Christopher Dorner's case.

Indeed, it is only now, after the damage has been done and Dorner himself has left this life, that his case is being reopened to review whether Dorner's initial claims of cover-up and racial discrimination had held any merit at all. It still remains to be seen if Dorner's claims of race playing a significant part in his 2008 dismissal are correct or not, and the truth is, that is something we may never find out.

Regardless of whatever the outcome of that new investigation turns out to be, truth is that mass shooters like Dorner always have some festering grievance against the world, whether it be related to ethnicity, gender, race, religion, romance, politics, economics, status or any other reason.

And like most people are prone to do, these mass murderers heap all their ire, resentment, bitterness and discontent onto the one factor or factors they believe to be responsible for their bad luck, neglect, suffering, humiliation, loss or mistreatment; be it parents, the government, teachers, spouses, bosses, technology, Wall Street or just society at large.

Apparently the thing that infuriated Christopher Dorner the most was the fact that he was losing position as a police officer, and that in his own eyes was equivalent to losing his good name or reputation.

In his bitter tirade online which later went on to be his manifesto, Dorner recalled the cases of Ted Kaczynski, the Unabomber and Norwegian mass murderer Anders Breivik. He reminisced about his childhood in Southern California and recounted that he grew up in an almost exclusively Caucasian neighborhood and school.

He mentions that his first encounter with racism was early in his childhood. He further describes how this racism followed him all his life and only increased during his brief time serving in the LAPD.

He believed that it was this racism, along with the unspoken thin blue line that bonds police departments in professional camaraderie and yet strongly discourages reporting bad behavior in any fellow police officer that led to his unfair dismissal from the officer, after he not only witnessed but formally documented the unfair use of cruel and excessive force by a senior training police officer during the arrest of a mentally ill person.

Judging from most accounts,

Christopher Dorner held himself and most others to a high moral standard, especially the police force who he thoroughly believed to be protectors rather than perpetrators.

Dorner was especially sensitive to and was aggressively vocal about racial discrimination. Judging from his manifesto, it was quite a disillusionment for Dorner to realize that such hurtful racism not only still lingers in the LAPD but also runs freely and affects people on a daily basis.

Here, countering this argument with the fact that America has not only elected but has also re-elected an African American as its president and to consider it equivalent to the eradication of racism in America is not only ludicrous but also rather delusional a thing to claim.

If we were to discuss the issue of racism, rage and mass murder, another case comes to mind, and that is the one of Colin Ferguson in New York City. In 1993, Ferguson who was a black man born and raised in Jamaica, calmly boarded a Long Island Rail Road car during rush hour commute and started shooting people.

This resulted in five deaths and eighteen people being wounded. Ferguson did not try to commit suicide as many other mass murderers are prone to do, either out of an embittered sense of despair, rage, hopelessness or in order to avoid having to face the consequences for the act they committed.

Not all mass murderers are suicidal, wanting to stick around and bask in the notoriety and infamy relished by their rage for recognition. In fact, many of them actively enjoy the chaos and suffering they create.

Looking at it from a traditional point of view, many mass murderers single out and target specific victims or at least victims that fit a specific profile, such as spouses, lovers, family members, co-workers, employees and the like, towards whom they wish to seek revenge to repay for some perceived or actual insult.

Others such as Seung Hui Cho at Virginia Tech, accused Batman shooter James Holmes in Colorado, and Anders Breivik in Norway make premeditated and meaningful choices about where, when and how to commit their crimes and don't care much about who the victim is as long as someone is unfortunate enough to be present there.

For example, once he was aboard the train, Ferguson's victims were selected more or less on impulse and haphazardly. Dorner's victims, on the other hand, were specifically listed and staked out and targeted.

He was waging quite skilled guerilla warfare against the individuals whom he believed had wronged him somehow. He was also going after their families as is apparent by the fact that he executed his defense counsel Ronald Quan's daughter, Monica Quan, along with her fiancé in their car.

He also targeted former Los Angeles police officers at large. Though he had ample opportunity to kill other individuals who were not related to law enforcement, he had chosen not to do so.

In this sense, the two crimes committed by Colin Ferguson and Christopher Dorner were rather different; however, both of these men had apparently been deeply wounded by the unfair system that put more weight in racism than it did in individuals.

Both these men, in short, had been disappointed by the system: Ferguson upon arriving in America as a naïve young man from his more privileged upbringing in Jamaica as well as Dorner who grew up in a predominantly white environment in Southern California and purportedly later as a rookie police officer in Los Angeles.

Both of these men were extremely frustrated and angry and felt tormented by their unfair fate. Both had allowed their rage to stew for some time. This period of stewing or festering is typically present in a mass murderer and can last from days to decades. It also makes up a key factor leading up to and driving their violent outbursts.

This can be regarded as a tragic example of what most people call chronic anger mismanagement. This anger mismanagement led both men to exact hateful and violent revenge on those they felt had wronged them, had impeded their progress in life or had stood in their way somehow.

Colin Ferguson, who was deemed to be depressed and psychotic at the time of the shootings, deliberately targeted middle-class Caucasians on a commuter train because they had been strangers who had been representatives of the 'American Dream' for him, a dream which he had never had for himself, and thus he deemed his victims the cause of his personal frustration, failure and disillusionment. He violently victimized the people he felt were victimizers.

Dorner was also likely depressed and embittered but not psychotic like Colin Ferguson. He had served as a former Navy reservist prior to joining the LAPD and had directly declared war on his former brethren who he had felt had betrayed and destroyed his life. Dorner was out for blood and retribution.

However, according to his own words, Christopher Dorner's motivation transcended mere revenge. His motivation was driven by a compulsive need to set the record straight, right a wrong and clear his name.

In his manifesto, he goes on about the meaning and importance of having a good name, of having a professional reputation, and the devastating effects of having his worth in life sullied and tarnished simply because of unfair racial practices.

This is something that concerns almost every human being at some point in their life because it is an existential fact of life that a person seldom possesses anything of worth other than his good name. And to have that hard-earned reputation and good name taken from you in the blink of an eye is something that can cause anyone to have a meltdown, especially if your name was tarnished over something as cruel as racial inequality.

Despite our best efforts to keep our reputations intact, we are all potentially susceptible to such a cataclysmic loss of what we hold so dear, precious and meaningful to us in our life. None of us can say with any certainty how dear our name is to us and how we would react to such a profound sort of existential crisis of losing said name and especially when the reason is, at least in some parts, unfair, unjust and the product of racial discrimination.

Racism is rooted in a fundamental

fear and a defensive sort of resentment and hostility towards those we project our 'rejected' shadow upon. Due to our conditioning, more than anything else, our mind believes that the people we are being racist towards are somehow beneath us and are thus somehow rejected. We deem these people as 'others' and deem them different and inferior.

The demonic rage, racial animus and plain hatred that accompany these sentiments are the few social evils that America still faces, and these are the social evils that seem to be the most deeply rooted in society. However, here arises a crucial question of how someone, no matter who they are, black, white, brown, Muslim, Hindu, Jew, anyone, deals with such self-evident evils as well as the frustration, anger, and rage they are bound to provoke.

Colin Ferguson found his few remaining shreds of meaning after his world had been blown more or less away in hating white people whom he saw as prejudicially thwarting his way to economic success in the country, especially success he may have felt narcissistically entitled to.

This behavior is not uncommon in

xenophobes as well as members of the KKK. The reason behind this is that it is always easier to blame someone else for our problems, anger and failure than to face the music, as the term goes. From Ferguson's perspective, his victims symbolized the devils and the villains who had been, in his eyes, victimizing him all along.

Similarly, the righteous indignation that was showed by Chris Dorner about being dismissed by the LAPD somehow twisted itself into the shape of a one-man crusade to clean up the residual racism that still ran amok in the offices of the LAPD. However, even more meaningful and important than to clean up the department had been the point of clearing his ruined reputation as a good police officer.

"*I have exhausted all available means at obtaining my name back. I have attempted all legal court efforts within appeals at the Superior Courts and California Appellate courts. This is my last resort.*" It seems that Dorner had always wanted to be a policeman and that his self-esteem and sense of meaning and purpose in life had been closely linked to having finally attained this dream.

Of course, when that dream shattered, Dorner's violent reign of terror became his sole sense of power as well as his biggest sense of purpose in life, i.e. it was the one thing that kept him going. Dorner was undoubtedly deeply wounded by his treatment by the department and had written in his manifesto that he admitted that he had fallen into a deep state of severe depression after he had been fired.

In any case, it is almost confirmed that what happened to Dorner had been a massive narcissistic injury that had resulted in the immense narcissistic rage of the wounded. Psychoanalyst Heinz Kohut (1978) defines narcissistic rage as "*The need for revenge, for righting a wrong, for undoing a hurt by whatever means, and a deeply anchored, unrelenting compulsion in the pursuit of all of these aims, which give no rest to those who have suffered a narcissistic injury--these are the characteristic features of narcissistic rage in all its forms and which sets it apart from other kinds of aggression.*"

Here arises the question of whether Dorner met the profile for Narcissistic

Personality Disorder. The answer to that is: not necessarily. Dorner had been reportedly bullied as a child and had been hurt and angered by racial taunts.

The general impression one gets of Christopher Dorner from reading his manifesto, watching interviews of the people who were close to him such as girlfriends, family, friends and co-workers is that Dorner had been a sensitive and idealistic person.

He was somewhat rigid and one could go far as to say dogmatic in his sense of right and wrong. His ex-girlfriend reported that there had been phases where Dorner went between being 'good Chris' and 'bad Chris.' This can be easily pinpointed into being something that Carl Jung calls a shadow or a person's dark side which exists in everyone but does not manifest dominantly in a lot of people.

Of course, it was something that manifested itself dominantly in Dorner himself as was evident by his fury and the path he took himself later on in life. At the end, it seems that Dorner had become a man of high moral and principles who had been unable to come to grips with his own raging demons of resentment.

He had been someone who felt victimized by evil but, lacking any constructive solution, had taken the path of fighting evil with evil and fire with fire. When we take a look at the manifesto, we see Dorner describe his actions as a necessary evil and thus come to the conclusion that he, like many other serial killers and mass murderers, had been in a dangerous state of mind for a period of time prior to his killing spree.

Calling his actions a necessary evil hints upon the fact that until the very end, Dorner had been well aware of what is right and what is wrong and had been able to differentiate between good and evil himself.

As has been witnessed in the cases of Colin Ferguson, Adam Lanza, Anders Breivik and other mass murderers or serial killers, Dorner could find no way out of the problem he found himself in, at least no productive way. Dorner could not contend with his frustration, disillusionment, anger and rage constructively and did not seek any professional help to get him through the ordeal either, as far as records tell us.

It is a sad fact that denying or repressing rage only tends to intensify it over a period of time which makes it all the more dangerous. The tragic result in both cases is a catastrophic detonation of destructive violence, and even though violence is not the answer in any way, it can be understood as an eruption of pent-up passion, an explosion of the drive to destroy what can be seen as the barrier to a person's self-esteem, movement and growth.

No one is immune to anger and almost everyone is susceptible to feelings of rage, anger and violent fantasies that usually accompany such dark thoughts. However, what differentiates between the majority of the world and the likes of Colin Ferguson, Seung Hui Cho, Anders Breivik, Adam Lanza or the Christopher Dorners of the world is the fact that a majority of us do not, as Shakespeare put it in Hamlet, 'take arms against a sea of troubles.' Of course, this is the last desperate stance of the troubled and embittered mass shooter.

In conclusion, the fact to be emphasized is that all of these murderers did not wake up one day and decide to kill every white person they saw. Behind these people is a history of oppression, both on a small and personal scale as well as on a larger and more historical perspective.

Dorner grew up in the midst of a white-heavy environment and thus became exposed to racial bullying at a very young age, and from a very young age, his mind had been exposed to hate since children of color are usually the first victims of bullying in any environment, especially one where the white population is heavier and greater in numbers. The whole Christopher Dorner saga could have been well avoided had the system been accustomed to checks and balances on every scale that makes sure that racial prejudice gets stopped and ultimately eradicated.

The thing to remember is that, in the end, Dorner did not get even a small percentage of the reward he had set out to get. He died in infamy and his retaliatory tactics did not redeem his reputation as he had hoped they would. In fact, he had completely destroyed his reputation long before his death because even if he had not been a liar, he had become a killer.

Here arises the question of whether

his death will play any part in the reformation and improvement of the LAPD as he had allegedly intended in the first place. There is some hope that the police will learn a lesson from this and will learn to set aside racial prejudices whilst handling criminals or even potential criminals.

The LAPD has a long history of both racial discrimination and excessive use of force against the people it is supposed to be serving, and this is as good an opportunity as any to make amends.

Thank you to my editor, proofreaders, and cover artist for your support:

~ RJ

Aeternum Designs (book cover), Bettye McKee (editor), Lee Knieper Husemann, Lorrie Suzanne Phillippe, Marlene Fabregas, Darlene Horn, Ron Steed, Katherine McCarthy, Robyn MacEachern, Kathi Garcia, Linda H. Bergeron

About the Author

RJ Parker, Ph.D. is an award-winning and bestselling true crime author and owner of RJ Parker Publishing, Inc. He has written over 20 true crime books which are available in eBook, paperback and audiobook editions, and have sold in over 100 countries. He holds certifications in Serial Crime, Criminal Profiling and a PhD in Criminology.

To date, RJ has donated over 3,000 autographed books to allied troops serving overseas and to our wounded warriors recovering in Naval and Army hospitals all over the world. He also donates to Victims of Violent Crimes Canada.

If you are a police officer, firefighter, paramedic or serve in the military, active or retired, RJ gives his eBooks freely in appreciation for your service.

Contact Information

Author's Email:

AuthorRJParker@gmail.com

Publisher's Email:

Agent@RJParkerPublishing.com

Website:

http://m.RJPARKERPUBLISHING.com/

Twitter:

http://www.Twitter.com/realRJParker

Facebook:

https://www.Facebook.com/AuthorRJParker

Amazon Author's Page:

rjpp.ca/RJ-PARKER-BOOKS

** SIGN UP FOR OUR MONTLY NEWSLETTER **

http://rjpp.ca/RJ-PARKER-NEWSLETTER

References

ALBERT FISH

https://prezi.com/fokbth5f-9ic/interview-with-albert-fish/

http://murderpedia.org/male.F/f/fish-albert.htm

TED BUNDY

http://murderpedia.org/male.B/b1/bundy-ted-citations.htm

https://vault.fbi.gov/Ted%20Bundy%20/

https://web.archive.org/web/20060621144017/http://tedbundy.com/errata/freebies/Ted%20Bundy%20Multiagency%20Investigative%20Team%20Report%201992%20from%20tedbundy.com.pdf

DENNIS NILSEN
Coffey, Russell (2013). *Dennis Nilsen: Conversations with Britain's Most Evil Serial Killer*. John Blake. ISBN 978-1-782-19459-0.

http://murderpedia.org/male.N/n/nilsen-dennis.htm

JEFFREY DAHMER
Blundell, Nigel (1996). *Encyclopedia of Serial Killers*.

PRC Publishing. ISBN 978-1-856-48328-5.

http://www.biography.com/people/jeffrey-dahmer-9264755

GARY RIDGWAY
http://www.biography.com/people/gary-ridgway-10073409

http://murderpedia.org/male.R/r/ridgway-gary.htm

http://crime.about.com/od/serial/a/Gary-Ridgway.htm

EDMUND KEMPER
Vronsky, Peter (2004), *Serial Killers: The Method and Madness of Monsters*, ISBN 0-425-19640-2

https://www.psychologytoday.com/blog/wicked-deeds/201403/the-real-life-horror-tale-the-twisted-co-ed-killer

1   http://www.policebrutality.info/2014/03/cops-who-shot-innocent-women-will-be-sent-back-into-field.html

2   https://en.wikipedia.org/wiki/Christopher_Dorner_shootings_and_manhunt

3   http://murderpedia.org/male.D/d/dorner-christopher.htm

4   https://factreal.wordpress.com/2013/02/08/manifesto-of-cop-killer-chris-dorners-full-text/

5   http://www.democraticunderground.com/101655176

6   http://www.pbs.org/wgbh/pages/frontline/shows/lapd/scandal/

7   https://www.researchgate.net/profile/William_Smith57/publication/247752199_Assume_the_Position_._._._You_Fit_the_DescriptionPsychosocial_Experiences_and_Racial_Battle_Fatigue_Among_African_American_Male_College_Students/links/54ef02da0cf2e55866f3daf4.pdf

8   http://www.latimes.com/nation/la-na-frein-manhunt-20141027-story.html

Printed in Poland
by Amazon Fulfillment
Poland Sp. z o.o., Wrocław